Adolescence

Recent Titles in
Contributions in Psychology

ADOLESCENCE

Biological and Psychosocial Perspectives

Benjamin B. Wolman

Contributions in Psychology, Number 35

GREENWOOD PRESS
Westport, Connecticut • London

Library of Congress Cataloging-in-Publication Data

Wolman, Benjamin B.
    Adolescence : biological and psychosocial perspectives / Benjamin
B. Wolman.
      p. cm.—(Contributions in psychology, ISSN 0736–2714 ; no.
35)
    Includes bibliographical references and index.
    ISBN 0–313–30311–8 (alk. paper)
    1. Adolescent psychology. I. Title. II. Series.
BF724.W65   1998
305.235—dc21   97–14466

British Library Cataloguing in Publication Data is available.

Library of Congress Catalog Card Number: 97–14466
ISBN: 0–313–30311–8
ISSN: 0736–2714

First published in 1998

Greenwood Press, 88 Post Road West, Westport, CT 06881
An imprint of Greenwood Publishing Group, Inc.

Printed in the United States of America

The paper used in this book complies with the
Permanent Paper Standard issued by the National
Information Standards Organization (Z39.48–1984).

10 9 8 7 6 5 4 3 2 1

Contents

Acknowledgment

I am most grateful to my editorial assistant, Mr. Paul Boyer, for his devoted and efficient help.

Benjamin B. Wolman

PART I

Patterns of Development

CHAPTER 1

Research Perspectives

In 1965 I was one of the invited speakers at the "Conference on Adolescence," presented by the International Association of Social Psychiatry. Because the conference took place in London, most of the participants were British psychiatrists and psychologists, but there were many experts in other fields and from other countries.

The views expressed at the conference were highly diversified. Some participants defended the recapitulation theory of G.S. Hall (1904). Others stressed Hall's view of adolescence as a "storm and distress" period. Biologically oriented experts focused on the physiology of pubertal changes, and some social psychiatrists and social psychologists viewed the "rebellion of youth" as a positive, sociocultural phenomenon that augured a better future for humanity. The amount of research work was rather sparse.

The years 1966 to 1968 witnessed a spectacular qualitative and quantitative upsurge of research works, longitudinal studies, and comprehensive surveys related to adolescence; suffice it to mention here the California and Fels Longitudinal Studies, among many others. In the 1970s several research workers stressed the need for a more thorough analysis of the transition from childhood to adolescence (Hamburg, 1974; Lipsitz, 1977). A great number of research works and encyclopedic reviews appeared in the 1970s and 1980s, among them Adelson, 1980; Coates, Petersen, and Perry, 1982; Conger and Petersen, 1984; Jessor and Jessor, 1979; Kandel and Lesser, 1972; Keating and Clark, 1980; Lerner and Foch, 1987; Magnusson, 1987; Offer and Offer, 1975; Petersen and Hamburg, 1986; Rutter, 1980; Santrock, 1987; Steinberg, 1985; Van Hasselt and Hersen, 1987; Wolman, 1982a; Wolman, Egan, and Ross, 1978; and numerous other works.

In 1988, *The Annual Review of Psychology* published a comprehensive review of research on adolescence (Petersen, 1988), the first of its kind devoted entirely to that subject.

There has been a highly diversified approach to research methods and conceptual systems, such as the ecological approach (Bronfenbrenner, 1979), the life-span developmental psychology (Baltes, Reese, and Lipsitt, 1980), psychoanalytic interpretation (Blos, 1979), and psychopathological research (Rutter, 1980; Rutter, Izard, and Read, 1986; Weiner and Del Gaudio, 1976). In April 1992 the Carnegie Corporation of New York and the Carnegie Council on Adolescent Development held in Washington, D.C., a national conference called "Crossroads: Critical Choices for the Development of Healthy Adolescents." The conference found that, "in 1989, 67 percent of all births to teenagers occurred out of wedlock, compared with 30 percent in 1970. . . . More adolescents before the age of fifteen are experimenting with illegal drugs and consume alcoholic beverages regularly" (*Carnegie Quarterly*, Vol. XXXVI, No. 4, p. 3).

In 1993 the American Psychological Association published *Special Issue: Adolescence* of the *American Psychologist*, edited by Ruby Takanishi. According to Takanishi,

> Adolescents today face greater risks to their current and future health than ever before. More adolescents are experimenting with drugs at a young age, especially before age 15. . . . Depression can affect between 7% and 33% of adolescents, depending on its definition, assessment and severity. . . . Suicide rates almost tripled among 10- to 14-year-olds between 1968–1985. . . . Homicide deaths among African-American males between 15 and 19 years of age increased 111% between 1985 and 1990.

As will be described in the following chapters, the biological age of maturity has not changed much. Males and females reach biological aspects of maturity more or less at the same time their ancestors did. However, the discrepancy between the biological aspects and the psychosocial aspects of maturity continues. Small wonder that the adolescent years are the years of difficulties and conflicts between the social roles of childhood and adulthood. Contemporary adolescents are biologically adult and tend to act as adults, but their sociocultural development does not prepare them for adult life. Adolescence is a period of normal maladjustment.

CHAPTER 2

Adolescence as a Biological Phenomenon

Children are born helpless, and their survival depends on the care and protection given to them by their parents and/or other adults. Childhood is a period of *dependence*; children's needs for food, shelter, protection, and love are met by their parents. The fear of abandonment is the most severe of all children's fears, and parental protection is a prerequisite of their physical and mental well-being.

Adults are *interdependent*, and their self-supporting activities necessitate interaction with other adults. Adults exchange goods and services; the shoemaker needs the baker's bread, and the baker needs shoes. Adults form networks, communities, and organizations that provide protection, health care, and economic ties.

Where do adolescents belong? They have outgrown the need for continuous parental care, but they are not yet ready for sharing adult responsibilities. They don't want to be dependent on their parents, but they are unable to take part in the interdependent system of adulthood. They rebel against childhood dependence, but before they reach interdependence they crave independence and tend to be rebellious (Coleman, 1974; Nesselrode and Baltes, 1979; Rutter, 1980).

The transition from childhood to adulthood is an uneven, often disharmonious process of *biological maturation*, complicated by sociocultural factors. Adolescence always represents a transition from childhood to adulthood, with a great many inevitable, related problems. Contemporary adolescence is also a transition from traditional educational methods and a conservative value system toward a rapidly changing, technological, and highly complex social system. Today's adolescents are exposed to a changing sociocultural environment superimposed upon the biological process of change.

Adolescence is a developmental phase of human life. Some aspects of adolescence are determined by biochemical processes common to all human beings. These are the basic, natural laws of transition from prenatal life, childbirth, infancy, and childhood through adolescence, young adulthood, middle age, and into old age. No human being goes through the same biological and psychological changes. Environmental, physical, and psychosocial factors may considerably affect the course of physical and psychological growth.

All adolescents undergo biological and psychological changes determined by the glands of inner secretion and other factors, but not all adolescents undergo the same physical and mental changes. The question is: To what extent do the various cultural settings and family relationships facilitate a smooth transition from one phase of life to the next, or to what extent do they contribute to maladjustment?

One may view adolescence in a life-span perspective proposed by Baltes (1973), and defined as follows:

> Life-span oriented view of human development deals with the study of long-term sequences and patterns of change in human behavior. The sequences and patterns may be studied as 1) interindividual differences in long-term sequences and patterns of intraindividual changes, or 2) long-term sequences and patterns of changes in interindividual differences. (Labouvie, 1982, p. 55)

Several researchers pointed to the discrepancy between the biochemical time span of adolescence and the impact of sociocultural influences. As will be described in detail on the following pages, adolescence is a period of physical maturation that does not produce simultaneous psychosocial maturation. However, Hall's (1904) idea of an alleged universal stormy transition from childhood to adulthood was questioned by Hollingsworth (1928), and anthropological research did not support the idea of stormy transitions (Mead, 1949, 1970). The growth in body size, weight, and sexual maturation does not correspond to the ability to earn a living and participate in mature, social responsibilities at a time of far-reaching technological and sociopolitical change. A host of contemporary researchers dealt with the complex problems of adolescent development in a highly complex social environment (Adelson, 1980; Blos, 1979; Bronfenbrenner, 1979; Coates, Petersen, and Perry, 1982; Jessor and Jessor, 1979; Petersen, 1988; Rutter, 1980; Simmons and Blyth, 1988; Wolman, 1982a; and others), and there are still a great many unanswered questions.

One of the questions asks: Is the gap between biological development and the sociopsychological readiness to join the adult society the same in all periods, or is it growing or declining in our period? Research offers rather inconclusive results depending on the choice of samples and diversity in research methods (Offer and Offer, 1975; Petersen, 1988). Some longitudinal studies try to take into consideration both biology and social psychology as well as the intraindividual and interindividual sequences and patterns of change (Nesselrode and Baltes, 1979), but the question is still open.

ENDOCRINOLOGICAL CHANGES

Psychoendocrinological research was started in 1849 by the German scientist A.A. Bertold, who studied testicular secretions in animals. Research on human subjects was started by the French scientist C.E. Brown-Sequard, who in 1899 reported to the *Societe de Biologie* that, in his seventies, he injected himself with animal testicular extracts and the injection rejuvenated him. In the early 1920s the Spanish scientist Gregorio Maranon conducted experimental research with adrenaline on human subjects. The research work of the American scientists W.B. Cannon, Hans Selye, and, more recently, J.W. Mason have opened new vistas in the relationship between the glands of inner secretion and psychology. At the present time the research is widely spread and offers new perspectives into the understanding of biological and psychological development (Baltes, Reese, and Lipsitt, 1980; Williams, 1979; and others). In addition, there is a growing body of research devoted to the role of the immune system, its interaction with the nervous system, and the glands of inner secretion (Ader, 1981; Raine, 1988).

Undoubtedly, the biochemical changes in early adolescence are brought about by hormones secreted by the endocrine glands. As soon as the hypothalamus of the brain starts to send impulses to the pituitary gland, the anterior lobe of the pituitary begins to secrete gonadotropic hormones, called *follicle stimulating hormones* (FSH), *luteinizing hormones* (LH), often called *interstitial cell stimulating hormones* (ICSH), and *luteotropic hormones* (LTH), often called prolactin or lactogenic hormones. The FSH, in cooperation with the LH, stimulate the growth of the ovarian follicles and cause ovulation and secretion of estrogen in females. In males the FSH foster the growth of the seminiferous tubules of the testes. The other cells of the testes, the secretion of androgen, and the production of sperm are stimulated by the LH (Cheek, 1974; Grumbach, Grave, and Mayer, 1974; Hamburg, 1974; Lerner and Foch, 1987).

The pituitary also secretes other hormones, namely *adrenotropin*, which controls the function of the adrenal gland; *thyrotropin*, which controls the thyroid gland; and *somatotropin*, which stimulates the growth of bones and tissues. In a case of inadequate (hypofunction) or excessive (hyperfunction) secretion of somatotropin, the functions of other glands are affected and the entire body chemistry can be seriously disturbed. An excessive secretion of somatotropic hormones produces rapid growth and may lead to *acromegaly* (gigantic dimensions of the body); an inadequate secretion may cause *dwarfism*. The speed and growth in adolescence and the ultimate results of body growth are greatly influenced by somatotropin (Falkner and Tanner, 1979).

The action of the somatotropic hormone is inhibited by the *gonadal hormones*. An abundant secretion of hormones by the ovaries and testes that signals puberty inhibits physical growth and brings it to a gradual stop. The males and females who had early puberty are usually small in stature. The gonadotropic hormones stimulate the development of the sex glands (gonads), that is, ovaries in females and testes in males. The gonadotropic hormones create the primary and secondary sexual characteristics in males and females (Hart, 1974).

The hormonal secretion may cause surprising developmental changes; an inadequate stimulation of male or female gonads by the gonadotropic hormones may affect one's bodily structure and produce an abnormal physical development. The production of sex hormones (estrogen in females and testosterone in males) is stimulated and regulated by the two anterior pituitary hormones, the FSH and the LH. High levels of these two hormones before puberty accelerate the maturation of the gonads and increase the production of estrogen and testosterone (Chumlea, 1982; Winter, 1978).

The testosterone stimulates a continuous production of sperm. The estrogen stimulates the maturation of the ovum once every 28 days. The levels of FSH rise at the beginning of every cycle and produce a considerable increase in secretion of estrogen, and consequently bring about the maturation of the follicles of the ovaries and a thickening of the endometrium of the uterus.

Both the LH and the FSH reach their peak at ovulation. The increased production of LH causes a rupture of the follicle, which enables the ovum to descend into the fallopian tubes, and the fertilized ovum becomes implanted in the wall of the uterus. After the descent of the ovum, the follicle forms the *corpus luteum* and begins to produce *progesterone* and *estrogen* (Brooks-Gunn and Petersen, 1983; Money, 1980; Wolman and Money, 1980).

PHYSICAL GROWTH

One of the outstanding signs of the onset of adolescence is the "growth spurt" which starts in girls around 10–11 years of age, reaches its peak around ages 12–13, and slows down substantially at age 14. In boys it starts around 12–13 years of age and reaches its peak around age 15–16; thus 10–13-year-old girls are usually taller than boys, but around the age of 15–16 boys surpass girls in height.

Increases in height are gradually decelerated from the prenatal life through infancy to childhood, then become accelerated at early adolescence and decline in late adolescence. The average increases in height for American white and black children are 50 percent in the first year of life, 16 percent in the second year, and below 4 percent before the child reaches 10 years of age. In early adolescence the annual increases in height are 5 to 8 percent. Girls after age 15 and boys after age 17 gain less than one percent annually.

One cannot predict the velocity of growth at adolescence. Children born tall may attain their growth spurt later than children born short and vice versa. Sometimes children who were comparatively tall at the age of 8–10 are outdistanced at age 12–14 by their classmates, and sometimes children who were short at the age of 12 become tall a few years later (Chumlea, 1982).

There are different growth rates for the head, the limbs, and so on. The height of the body measured from the vertex of the head to the soles of the feet is usually divided into three main components, namely the head and neck, the trunk, and the lower limbs. The head and the neck at birth form 25 percent of body length, the trunk 39 percent, and the lower limbs 36 percent. At the age of 12 the length of the lower limbs reaches 48 percent of body stature for girls. At the age of 14 the lower limbs are 49 percent of body stature in boys, while the head and neck size is reduced to less than 19 percent (Tanner, 1974).

The velocity of growth for the various parts of the body is not correlated at all. For a while some adolescents may have short trunks, long lower limbs, and average heads and necks, and after a year or two they may look entirely different. There are all possible combinations of velocity of growth of the various body parts, and quite often adolescents wonder about their appearance and worry about the impression they make on others. On the average the head of a 15–16-year-old boy has reached its adult size, but the upper and lower limbs continue to grow. In most cases the skeletal growth comes to an end in 16–17-year-old girls and in 20–21-year-old boys (Roche, 1979; Sinclair, 1978).

WEIGHT

Increases in bodily weight follow a complex pattern. The average American newborn boy weighs 7.7 pounds, the average girl 4 to 5 percent less. The body weight at age 1 is three times greater than at birth. The increases in weight gradually slow down in early childhood, remain relatively constant in middle childhood, accelerate in early adolescence, and decline in late adolescence. The acceleration for girls starts two years earlier than for boys.

The average American (white and black), British, Norwegian, and Czechoslovak 13-year-old girls weigh about 100 pounds, as compared to below 80 pounds for Chinese, Burmese, and African girls of the same age. The average 15-year-old American, Swedish, and Australian boys weigh about 120 pounds, as compared to below 80 pounds for Egyptian, Bantu, and Indian boys of the same age (Evleth and Tanner, 1976).

The typical differences in weight are related to nutrition rather than to race. Ninety years ago the average North American white male was lighter in weight by five pounds at the age of 5, thirty pounds at the age of 15, and fifteen pounds at the age of 20.

In most instances newborn girls have more subcutaneous fat than newborn boys. The differences in the total amount of body fat begin to grow from the age of 6 years on, and become quite significant at adolescence, when the fat layer in girls increases in their breasts, thighs, and buttocks (Malina, 1978).

THE INNER ORGANS

At the age of 6 the heart is four to five times as heavy as it was at birth, and at 12 it is almost seven times as heavy. During adolescent years the heart doubles in size and weight, but the growth of the heart and of the arteries and veins is rather uneven.

There are also substantial changes in the functions of the heart. There is a distinct though uneven rise in blood pressure. At puberty the blood pressure is higher in girls than in boys, but after 13 years of age the blood pressure in boys exceeds that of girls and keeps growing for a few years. At the end of the teenage years the blood pressure in boys is usually higher than in girls.

The lungs grow considerably during adolescence, with boys exceeding girls in size, weight, and lung capacity. This process of growth comes to an end at around age 17 in girls and around age 20 in boys (Roche, 1979).

This speedy physical growth necessitates enormous amounts of calories, and practically all adolescents have voracious appetites, especially during the growth periods.

PHYSICAL STRENGTH

Adolescent boys are physically stronger than girls, and the differences increase with age. Girls grow physically strong for a few years and then level off at about 16 to 18 years of age. The physical strength of boys increases rapidly. The bones and muscles of the trunk, hands, arms, and shoulders grow in strength, and the difference between the physical strength of 16–18-year-old boys and girls is quite considerable (Carron and Bailey, 1974).

There are also quite significant differences between boys and girls in regard to motor coordination. The agility and speed of movement in girls increases up to the age of 14–16 and then tapers off. The fact that girls mature earlier than boys may in some instances give girls a temporary edge over boys. Some 14-year-old girls have better motor coordination than boys at the same age, and in many instances somewhat older girls perform as well as or better than boys. However, toward the end of the teenage years boys' motor coordination is superior to that of girls (Malina, 1978).

PUBERTY IN FEMALES

Maturation in females is characterized by the growth of pubic hair, increases in the size of breasts, ovaries, and uterus, and the onset of menstruation, called menarche. The breasts begin to enlarge around the age of 10½, and it takes about three years before they reach their full size. The development of breasts and pubic hair may start anytime from about four years ahead of menarche up to soon after the onset of menarche. Menarche causes substantial deceleration in physical growth.

There are widespread variations in the age of onset of menstruation. About 95 percent of white and black American girls begin to menstruate between the ages of 10 and 16 years, 50 percent between the ages of 12 and 14, and 2 percent after age 16. There are also some cases of premature menstruation prior to the age of 6 and late menstruation after the age of 20. The average age of menstruation in the United States is about 13, and approximately the same for French, German, British, Australian, Russian, Hungarian, and Polish girls (Wolman and Money, 1980).

Menarche rarely signifies the beginning of procreation. It usually takes about one to three years from the onset of menstruation before girls develop the ability to conceive.

There is an impressive body of evidence that at the present time people reach biological maturity at an earlier age than their parents and much earlier than their grandparents. This phenomenon, called the "secular trend," has been observed in the United States and all over Europe. In Norway, for example, the average age of menarche was 17 years in 1840, 15½ years in 1900, and 13 at the present time. In the United States, the average age of menarche in 1900 was 14 years, and today it is somewhat below 13 years of age. It is likely that better nutrition and better health have accelerated the process of physical development (Roche, 1979).

PUBERTY IN MALES

The seminal vesicles, the prostate, the genital passages, and the penis are the primary male sexual signs. The growth of testes begins at about 10–11 years of age but does not become rapid until about 13–14 years, and reaches its peak by around 17 years. Prostate activity starts at the age of 11–12, and pubic hair grows at the age of 12–13. Axillary and upper lip hair starts growing at the age of 14–15. The penis grows in association with the enlargement of the testes, and it takes about five years from the initial increase of velocity to the attainment of full size. The age of onset of penal growth is between 10–15 years; the average age of onset of rapid growth of testes and penis is 13–14 years. Between the ages of 13 and 17 the size of the penis doubles, and between the ages of 12 and 19 the size of the testes grows tenfold. The production of sperm may start at any time between the ages of 11 and 17, and full sexual maturity is attained when the general growth has begun to slow down but has not fully ceased. In some boys the penis, scrotum, pubic, and axillary hair may reach full development at 15 years of age, and in others not earlier than the age of 20.

Boys usually attain the peak of physical growth between the ages of 17 and 20 and girls between 15 and 18. Boys reach their maximum physical strength at about age 20, girls at around age 16. The osseous development in boys is completed at 19–20, in girls about two or three years earlier. The peak of motor abilities in boys is about 18, in girls about 15. The average age of discharge of motile spermatozoa in boys is about 15, and the average age of ovulation in girls is 13. The growth of sexual organs and secondary sexual traits is completed in boys around the age of 17–19, and in girls around 15–17. One may safely conclude that boys at the age of 17–20 and girls 16–18 are biologically as mature as they could ever be (Brooks-Gunn and Petersen, 1983; Green and Horton, 1982; Katchadourian, 1977; Money, 1980).

EARLY AND LATE MATURATION

Early physical maturation, especially the height and appearance of secondary physical traits, such as a moustache in boys, offers certain advantages in interaction with peers. Tall, athletic boys are more popular with other boys and even more popular with girls, while late-maturing boys who are shorter than their age-mates are often looked down at and made to feel less "manly" than the others. To be short, beardless, and have a childlike physical appearance may adversely affect a boy's self-esteem and self-confidence, whereas the early maturing, tall boys who grow facial hair may feel that they have already reached maturity and therefore act in a self-confident manner (Marshall and Tanner, 1970; Siegel, 1982). However, in some instances slow-maturing boys have a better chance at keeping pace with their own psychosocial development. Slow biological maturation may reduce the gap between physical and mental growth, and late physical maturation could facilitate the development of perception, intellectual, and motor skills in a rather conflict-free setting (Petersen and Crockett, 1985).

The age of menarche is usually earlier in girls who belong to higher socioeconomic classes. Severe malnutrition can adversely affect the age of bodily growth and maturation. Precocious puberty is related to genetic factors.

The psychological implications of early maturation are less pronounced for females, although in some instances early-maturing girls are exposed to socially disadvantageous situations. Girls mature earlier than boys, and early-maturing girls who are taller than their peers are often ridiculed and even ostracized. However, these differences and difficulties gradually disappear, and early-maturing girls usually make adequate social adjustments (Marshall and Tanner, 1970; Zelnik and Kantner, 1980).

A connection has been found linking unusually high levels of adrenal androgen to a disordered period of adjustment in both male and female adolescents. This finding is significant due to the fact that levels of adrenal androgen can vary with the presence of stress-producing factors in the environment.

Advancing into puberty has strong implications for adolescents as they enter a higher social status and deal with an emerging sexuality. Social and cultural factors related to feminine beauty have been tied to the connection between puberty and inadequate image of one's body that appears frequently in girls (Faust, 1983; Garner and Garfinkel, 1980). For boys, hormones are more often implicated in emerging sexuality (Meyer-Bahlburg et al., 1985) and in aggression (Olweus, 1979; Susman et al., 1987). In most respects adolescents are pleased with the pubertal changes they undergo, and the reported findings go a long way to dispel the stereotypical storm and stress of the adolescent years (Wolman and Money, 1993).

Individuation, defined as an equilibrating process between connectedness and individuality, has also been the subject of adolescent research with respect to family interaction (Cooper et al., 1983; Grotevant and Cooper, 1985, 1986). Connectedness is defined as having two components: (1) mutuality, which implies a sensitivity to the emotions and needs of others, and (2) permeability, which implies opening oneself to the influences of others. Individuality, on the other hand, is characterized as a blend of separateness, which requires the maintaining of a suitable distance between oneself and others in terms of emotions and opinions, and self-assertion, which is the willingness to reveal one's thoughts and opinions to others. The connectedness and individuality of adolescents were subjected to a discourse analysis and drawn from the first 300 utterances within the family setting. Using high school seniors as their study group, Cooper and Grotevant found both components of individuation favorable for adolescent development (Cooper et al., 1983; Grotevant and Cooper, 1985).

A connection between enabling discourse and greater ego development has been made by Hauser (Hauser et al., 1984). Discourse that was less than enabling was tied to a lower level of ego development. The adolescent subjects' ego development and general structure of family interaction were also tied to the character of adolescent discourse, whether even or uneven.

CHAPTER 3

Intellectual Development

Intelligence has been defined as the ability to solve problems with the aid of symbols representing ideas and relationships. These symbols include words, numbers, diagrams, and equations. It is generally agreed that mental growth as measured by intelligence tests continues throughout the childhood years, and the IQ scores based on relationships between mental age and chronological age remain fully constant throughout the adolescent years (Flavell and Markman, 1983).

Mental functions do not mature at the same time. On the average, the top level of spatial perception and reasoning is reached around age 14, and the adult level of memory is usually attained at age 16. The average adolescent male or female reaches the peak of their intellectual development around 18–19 years of age. Mentally retarded individuals reach their peak much earlier and gifted individuals considerably faster (Wolman, 1985).

Genetic endowment is the main but certainly not the sole determinant of mental development. Adolescents who grow up in slum areas, in an inadequate home environment, or in any other anticultural environment might face serious obstacles in attaining full development of their potentialities. Obviously, genetic factors can make the offspring similar to or different from their parents, and the levels of intellectual achievements do not necessarily correspond to the levels attained by their parents. The relationship between heredity and environment and the impact of each of these two factors has been reported by several studies (Rainwater, 1970; Vandenberg and Vogler, 1985).

Intelligence and other mental functions are not totally independent from environmental influences. Even the best seed will not develop into a plant if it is put into arid soil. Good, innate potentialities are definitely the prime factor, but they may lead nowhere in a futile environment, and an early deprivation can prevent mental development.

There is a high correlation between environmental factors and intellectual achievement. Income is the highest single correlate of achievement, followed by occupation and education. However, it may well be that the parental education is a reasonable proxy for intelligence, and the intrinsic factors are to a large extent genetic, rather than environmental.

INTELLECTUAL PROCESSES

The assessment of intellectual processes in adolescence is a rather controversial issue. Inhelder and Piaget (1958) used fifteen tasks in an experimental study that illustrates the development of logical thinking and formal operational thought. Further research, reported by Neimark (1982), supported most aspects of Piaget's theory and pointed to significant changes in "the quality and power of thought" in adolescence, especially during the years from 11 to 15. Moreover, there is ample evidence that as the years go on, thought processes are undergoing significant development. Obviously the speed, the quality, and the range of intellectual development are influenced by formal education (Karplus, 1981; Keating and Clark, 1980; Simmons and Blyth, 1988).

There is a great variety in the levels of intellectual development that individual adolescents achieve, but this is true for any period of human life. The levels of intelligence and the individual differences in intellectual processes depend primarily on genetic factors (Vandenberg and Vogler, 1985). Some adolescents are mentally retarded, whereas others are highly gifted. One must, however, emphasize the role of the environment. The socioeconomic factors, educational experience, and family background can stimulate or hamper intellectual development (Goldberger, 1978; Rainwater, 1970). Moreover, the evolution of Piaget's theory and the modifications in measurement techniques have opened new vistas in interpretations of individual differences (Pascual-Leone, 1980).

Not all adolescents follow a single path of intellectual progress. The early years of adolescence are frequently years of lowering of school grades and often of unpredictable academic failure. The transition from the grade school into junior high school is often associated with failure in school grades and also with truancy and dropping out.

One need not assume a genuine intellectual decline. The early adolescent years do not cause a mental decline, but they often cause a serious decline in intellectual interest and in academic progress. Many adolescents lose faith in their intellectual abilities, and their academic motivation is substantially reduced. Their poor academic achievements discourage them, yet their poor self-perception does not reduce their wish to attend school and increase their scholastic efforts. The transition from grammar school into junior high school contributes to the above-mentioned difficulties (Simmons and Blyth, 1988). The change of the environment also plays a negative role in self-confidence and self-perception.

One might summarize the studies that follow Piaget's conceptual system as follows. Piaget (1965) and Inhelder and Piaget (1958) distinguished the following stages in the development of thought processes: the first two years form the "sensorimotor" phase, the ages 2–7 "preoperatory" or "preconceptual" thought, and between 7–11 years the child develops the ability for "concrete operations," such as classification, serialization, quantification, spatial perception, and so on. Around the ages of 11–15 the adolescent becomes capable of "formal operations," can use logical symbols, thinks in abstract terms, and becomes capable of analysis of theoretical concepts and formulation of hypotheses. The concern with the nature of the world and social order is typical for late adolescents. Many of them embrace radical political ideas and want to reform the world. Most 18-year-olds are capable of intellectual analysis of social and moral problems (Beilin, 1976; Feather, 1980).

Preadolescents tend to reason in somewhat dogmatic fashion, but the intellectual curiosity and increased ability of abstract thinking enables adolescents to think in a more flexible and open-minded manner. Dogmatic reasoning and belief in authorities typical for those aged 9–11 yields ground to skepticism and criticism of accepted values. Many adolescents turn away from organized religion, but some of them develop religious and mystical beliefs. Some adolescents abandon religion, others embrace it, though they may prefer a radically different version of what their parents believe in. Some adolescents convert or wish to convert to another religion. Many adolescents become concerned with the nature of the universe and man's destiny. Discussing religion, politics, morals, social order and, above all, their own personalities and future becomes the favorite pastime activity in adolescent groups (Hogan and Emler, 1978).

The intellectual changes in older adolescents enable them to understand social problems and partake in adult social relations. Adolescents' demand for equal rights, their craving for independence, and their criticism of the adult society and its social, economic, and political institutions are not a matter of hormonal imbalance and emotional immaturity. The improvement in cognitive processes enables adolescents to analyze social roles within the family group and the society at large and examine critically the discrepancies between justice as professed and as practiced (Lerner and Shea, 1982).

INTERESTS

The interests and hobbies of adolescents depend on their sociocultural background. In their striving to become adults, or at least give the impression of being mature, adolescents shy away from "kid stuff" and childish interests. Adolescents experiment with new situations that represent to them adult-like interests and attitudes, and they desire to become involved in a wide variety of interests and activities of positive value. In tradition-oriented societies adolescents imitate their parents' activities and occupations; for instance, in the past, adolescents in England strove to look and sound like lords and ladies in Eastern Europe; in Jewish communities, many adolescents displayed religious devotion (Rokeach, 1979).

The choice of interests in adolescence depends on many factors, such as level of education, sex, intelligence, family, social status, prestige value of different interests, peer group influence, and opportunities available for forming and engaging in various activities (Keating and Clark, 1980). Major interests of boys are outdoor sports requiring physical prowess, working on cars, listening to music and watching television, playing musical instruments, and belonging to peer groups. The interests of girls include outdoor sports and some of the same interests as listed above for boys. One of the more popular interests involves cars. Automobiles can serve many adolescent needs and purposes, such as giving the teenager a status symbol, increasing mobility, and providing privacy and excitement (McKinney, Hotch, and Trahon, 1977).

ACADEMIC ACHIEVEMENT

Academic achievement in adolescence depends on several factors, and IQ is only one of them. Sociocultural influences and parental attitudes may greatly influence scholastic progress. Some parents encourage intellectual achievement and foster intellectual independence. Studies of creative adolescents found a great deal of parental encouragement and guidance. Apparently, friendly and interested parents may help their children to do better in academic achievements than their classmates who have the same IQ but whose parents have shown no interest or have been critical and disrespectful of their children, their school, and their teachers. I have often had in psychotherapy gifted individuals who, in their adolescent years, gave up their creative work because of disparaging remarks made by parents or teachers (Wolman, 1982a).

Stanley Hall (1904) described the academic career of famous individuals as follows:

Wagner at the Nikolaischule at Leipzig was relegated to the third form, having already attained to the second at Dresden, which so embittered him that he lost all taste for philology and, in his own words, "became lazy and slovenly." Priestly never improved by any systematic course of study. W.H. Gibson was very slow and was rebuked for wasting his time sketching. James Russell Lowell was reprimanded, at first privately and then publicly, in his sophomore year "for general negligence in themes, forensics, and recitations," and finally suspended in 1838 "on account of continued neglect of his college duties." . . . Byron was so poor a scholar that he only stood at the head of the class when, as was the custom, it was inverted, and the bantering master repeatedly said to him, "Now, George, man, let me see how soon you'll be at the foot." Schiller's negligence and lack of alertness called for repeated reproof, and his final school thesis was unsatisfactory. Hegel was a poor scholar, and at the University it was stated "that he was of middling industry and knowledge but especially deficient in philosophy." . . . Heine agreed with the monks that Greek was the invention of the devil. "God knows what misery I suffered with it." He hated French meters, and his teacher vowed he had no soul for poetry. He idled away his time at Bonn, and was "horribly bored" by the "odious, stuffy, cut-and-dried tone" of the leathery professors. Humboldt was feeble as a child and "had less facility in his studies than most children." "Until I reached the age of sixteen," he says, "I showed little inclination for scientific pursuits." He was essentially self-taught, and acquired most of his knowledge rather late in life. At nineteen he had never heard of botany. . . . Swift was refused his degree because of "dullness and insufficiency," but given it later as a special favor. . . . Napoleon graduated forty-second in his class. "Who," asks Swift, "were the forty-one above him?" Darwin was "singularly incapable of mastering any language." When he left school, he says, "I was considered by all my masters and by my father as a very ordinary boy, rather below the common standard in intellect. To my deep mortification, my father once said to me, 'You care for nothing but shooting, dogs, and rat-catching, and you will be a disgrace to yourself and to all your family.'"

CHAPTER 4

Psychosocial Development and the Peer Group

All human behavior is related to the discharge of biochemical energy. At a certain evolutionary level, part of this energy is transformed into mental energy. The basic directness of all human actions is survival; human behavior is primarily focused on the protection of life.

This fundamental and universal drive, called *lust for life*, can be applied in a life-supporting and helping direction. One may then call it *Eros* (the Greek god of love), and the energy at its disposal *libido*. It may, however, also be used in a hostile and destructive direction, called *Ares* (the Greek god of war), and the destructive energy *destrudo*. Both libido and destrudo can be directed toward others and/or toward oneself (Wolman, 1973a).

The newborn child is narcissistic, that is, the entire libido is invested in oneself and the destrudo directed in self-defense against others. Both libido and destrudo serve survival purposes. As the child grows, his or her behavior can lead in four possible directions, usually hostile, and then friendly directions, namely instrumental, mutual, and vectorial.

Whenever one relates to others in order to have his or her needs satisfied, it is an *instrumental* attitude. When one wants to give and to get, it is *mutual*. The infant's attitude to the mother is instrumental, friendship and marriage mutual. Mature parents have a *vectorial* attitude toward their child; they are willing to give, expecting nothing in return.

Mature adults are capable of rational behavior in all four directions, namely (1) hostility, (2) instrumentalism, (3) mutualism, and (4) vectorialism. They can be *hostile* in self-defense, *instrumental* (takers) in the pursuit of livelihood, *mutual* (givers and takers) with friends, sex partners, and spouses, and finally *vectorial* (givers) toward their children and in charitable and idealistic activities (Wolman, 1974).

THE ANOMOUS PHASE

There are five distinct phases of social development from birth to maturity. The first phase is *anomous*. Human life begins in a state of extreme instrumentalism, and unlimited and unrestrained selfishness. Prenatal life is necessarily parasitic as the not-yet-born organism "lives off" its mother's body. After birth the survival of neonates depends upon their ability to continue the *parasitic-narcissistic* position of the prenatal life. *To take everything and to give nothing in return is the survival device of every newborn child*. At the initial stage of life there is no love for anyone except for oneself, and the infant's entire libido is invested in oneself. There are no restraints or inhibitions. The infant wants what he or she wants, and his or her needs must be taken care of instantly (Lewis and Rosenblum, 1974).

THE PHOBONOMOUS PHASE

The parents or parental substitutes usually relate to an infant in a vectorial way and supply food and protection in an affectionate and loving manner. The infant is a taker and puts into his mouth whatever is given to him, hence the psychoanalytic name: the *oral* stage.

The oral stage is an early form of instrumentalism, and the infants' desire to have their needs satisfied is associated with fear of abandonment and anger when they don't instantly get what they want (Freud, 1938; Osofsky, 1979). Infantile aggressiveness usually meets with parental restraints. When infants become aware of the overwhelming parental power, they enter a new phase in their psychosocial development, the phobonomous phase.

At the phobonomous phase the infants' desire to be taken care of and the wish to get whatever they want is associated with the fear of being rejected, and hostility when their needs are not taken care of. When the infants' wishes are turned down, they attack. According to Freud (1938, p. 28), "Sadistic impulses already begin to occur sporadically during the oral phase along with the appearance of teeth."

The oral stage is instrumental and hostile; it is phobonomous. The anal phase brings the ability to walk and to talk, and it increases the infants' feeling of power. The so-called "terrible *no* period" is a continuation of the phobonomous, instrumental, and hostile attitude. Psychoanalysts describe the infants' hostile attitude at toilet training and call this period "anal-sadistic." Obviously, the oral and the anal phases are phobonomous (Wolman, 1978a).

The need to be taken care of and the fear of abandonment lead the infant toward acceptance of parental authority, and the heteronomous phase begins (Freud, 1938;

Wolman, 1984a). At the new phase, the child surrenders to parental orders and develops the wish to gain parental love as well as the fear of losing it.

THE HETERONOMOUS PHASE

Social adjustment is predetermined by the ability to exercise emotional control over one's libido-love and destrudo-hatred impulses. The processes of growth and learning enable the child to give back some of the love that has been given to him or her by the parents. As a rule, children who have received plenty of parental love are better prepared to give love to others. At that time the child's attitude toward the parent of the opposite sex undergoes a deep metamorphosis (Freud, 1958).

The oedipal love for the mother leads to ambivalent feelings toward the father. The father is the main provider and satisfier of needs. If the father is perceived by the child as a strong (capable of satisfying needs) and friendly (willing to do so) person, the child wishes the strong and friendly father to be even stronger and friendlier. The oedipal conflict is a conflict between the desire to protect and to destroy, the conflict between love and hate. The child's attitude to the parent of the same sex is a combination of love and fear that leads to *identification with some-one the child loves and fears, which then leads to the formation of superego and of inner inhibition of hostile and sexual impulses.* Acceptance of separation-fear plays the leading role in motivating the child's behavior. Children at this age are jealous and possessive and become very dependent on parents. They resent sharing parental love with their siblings, and they try to please and conform (Wolman, 1978a).

THE SOCIONOMOUS PHASE AND THE PEER GROUP

The transition from identification with one's parents toward identification with one's peers is gradual, and for a while the one does not exclude the other. School-age children may be profoundly involved with their parents and at the same time form strong ties with one or a few close friends. Children's cliques develop various degrees of loyalty to one another and especially to the leader of the clique, and quite often the inner group bond leads to a hostile attitude toward outsiders. Some of the children's peer groups develop a secret language and have their own secret hideout unknown to parents and teachers. Belonging to a peer group gives their members the feeling of outgrowing childhood dependence on parents and, in many instances, gives the illusion of being independent and adult (Lerner and Shea, 1982; Youniss and Smollar, 1985).

As members of a peer group adolescents feel more self-confident, more courageous, and more outgoing. Belonging to a group enhances adolescents' self-image. They feel that they have more influence and have more to say as compared to single individuals. The peer group counteracts the feeling of loneliness, and peer pressure is a powerful motive for group identification and sharing the norms and values of the peers.

The peer groups rarely demand total uniformity, but an unswerving loyalty and a high degree of conformity with group manners and morals is typical for adolescent peer groups. In most instances, the adolescent's self-concept develops by accepting and sharing the group's ends and means and identifying with the members as a whole. Whereas at home the parents set the rules, the members of peer groups take an active part in setting the rules and accepting them as independent partners. Thus, they enter a new phase in personality development (Erikson, 1968). Instead of the parent-related superego, they develop the *we-ego*, that is, a willing sharing of thoughts and wishes with their peers (Wolman, 1984a).

The adolescent tendency to form peer groups is universal, but the nature of the groups is different in different countries. For instance, in the former Soviet Union, the formation of adolescent groups was encouraged by the government, and the adolescent groups were carriers of rules of allegiance to the Communist ideology. The socially accepted behavioral patterns and the loyalty to the Soviet government were transmitted and reinforced by the peer groups. In an Israeli kibbutz, the peer groups are based on strong, interpersonal, friendly ties, and they perform many functions usually performed by families. In the United States there are several types of peer groups. Some are formed in schools, but more of them in neighborhoods where the adolescents can see each other daily and "hang out" together on weekends. Some peer groups are related to a common ethnic background, but many of them serve as a melting pot for various religions, ethnic, and cultural backgrounds (Adler, 1977; Long, Henderson, and Pratt, 1973).

Most adolescents in the United States spend their leisure time not with their families, but with their peers. Often their goals in life and their behavior patterns are determined by peers, especially by the group leaders, usually athletic boys and popular girls. Parents and teachers are often ignored and overtly or covertly opposed as representing obsolete ideas of the "old times" and carriers of childhood dependence (Youniss and Smollar, 1985).

Boys like to spend a great deal of their time in active outdoor pursuits, such as sports or just "going around" with each other. They also spend time on hobbies, the most frequent of which is working on their cars, or on passive pursuits such as movies, television, and music. Contrary to what many adults sometimes think, spending time with girls does not constitute the major part of their leisure activities. It does, through the years, begin to occupy more time, however.

Girls' leisure-time activities show a distinct contrast in some categories. Their frequent activities include just being with friends, watching television and going to movies, attending games, and listening to music. Among their more active pursuits is dancing with each other. Probably dancing is a substitute for sports, but it is certainly preparation for dancing with boys.

Organized sports of both boys and girls have a direct relation to school, and some of the hobbies and other activities have their genesis in school. However, except for some hobbies and organized sports, school-related activities are not preferred leisure-time activities (Adams, 1979).

GROUP LEADERS

Adolescents often claim that their groups do not have leaders, but quite often their groups are referred to by the name of one of its members, who usually is the leader. Even when adolescents deny that they have a leader, there is always one individual who occupies the leadership position and plays an important role in relating the group to other groups and to the adult society. In fact, practically all adolescent groups and cliques develop a hierarchic status system.

The leader is usually more socially mobile than the followers, and consequently better informed about their activities. The leader is usually a coordinating and integrating figure in the social structure of the group. The leader is usually endowed with organizational skills required for the coordination of group activities, as well as with personality traits allowing him or her to mix freely with outsiders and maintain friendly relations within the group. In many instances, the leader guides the social behavior of the members of the group (Newman, 1982).

PARENTS AND TEACHERS

Most American parents try, with rather uneven results, to continue their guiding position with their adolescent sons and daughters. They are more successful when the adolescents form traditionally-oriented groups that promote parental ethnical, religious, or political values. However, in most instances adolescent groups develop their own sets of values quite different from their parents. These values, which can be viewed as a separate subculture, represent the second phase in social development, the first phase is dependence, the second is the adolescent craving for independence, and the third, the adult phase, is interdependence.

Whereas most parents do not favor peer groups, teachers and school administrators tend to accept them and usually refrain from bringing members of different peer groups into a working relationship with one another. In many instances the educators allow the groups to establish their boundaries and rivalries. Sometimes they encourage the formation of separate groups by assigning a certain group of students to certain tasks, such as record-keeping functions or monitoring the halls and assigning other groups to other tasks. Quite often the teachers rely on leaders of peer groups to help them to enforce certain patterns of behavior and impose school discipline on group members (Kandel and Lesser, 1972).

In most instances the school and peer group cooperation does not affect the set of values of adolescents. Most adolescent boys, in opposition to their parents and teachers, favor self-indulgence, personal pleasure, waiting for "good things to happen," seeking adventure, and fighting for one's whims and wishes. Most adolescent girls do not go that far in rejecting the values of parents and teachers, but they also are less concerned with honesty and truthfulness, and prefer waiting for "good things to happen" over hard work. As mentioned above, often boys and girls tend to conform with their peer groups more than their parents and teachers, even when they are members of school-supervised groups (Lidz, 1969; Steinberg, 1981; Lerner and Foch, 1987).

PEERS OR PARENTS?

The interaction between adolescents and their parents compared to adolescents' interaction with their peers is a controversial issue. Undoubtedly, adolescents tend to spend more time with their peers than with their parents, and as they grow older they move away from their parents and move closer to their peers. In terms of personality dynamics, they tend to become less dependent on their parents as they outgrow the heteronomous phase, and more interdependent with their peers as they move toward the socionomous, "we-ego" level (Wolman, 1973a). However, some constructive parental attitudes definitely help adolescents to adjust to adult life (Grotevant and Cooper, 1985).

The issue is far from being crystal-clear. Psychoanalytic studies stress the stormy relationship between adolescents and their parents because these studies are related to what psychoanalysts and other psychotherapists deal with in their clinical practice. In my own psychotherapeutic experience in hospitals and private practice I did not see anyone but rebellious, maladjusted adolescents and their maladjusted parents. Small wonder that psychoanalytic studies report the same experience (Adelson and Doehrman, 1980; Blos, 1970; Freud, 1958; and others).

It is still an open question how often adolescents and their parents are in conflict (Montemayer, 1983). Some researchers, to be mentioned later, maintain that adolescents have more in common with their parents than with their peers and tend to follow their parents' value system rather than their peers'. However, it is my impression that too many parents have little or no cultural or moral values, or are unable or unwilling to offer them to children, and the social climate of disinhibition and deculturation is at least partially responsible for belligerent, antisocial, and sociopathic behavior in many adolescents (Wolman, 1983, 1987).

According to data reported by Douvan and Adelson (1966), family relationships in adolescent are more influential than peer relationships. The 14- to 18-year-old boys and girls rarely have serious conflicts with their parents. Even the choice of their adolescent friends is influenced by parental attitudes, and they prefer to associate with peers whose behavior and value systems are acceptable to their parents. Similar views were reported by Kandel and Lesser (1972) and Smith (1976). However, adolescents tend to overestimate and parents tend to underestimate the extent of the difference between themselves (Blos, 1979; Grotevant and Cooper, 1983; Steinberg, 1981).

Are the conflicts between adolescents and parents growing or declining as our society progresses? According to Petersen (1988) the "adolescent versus the parent" conflict reaches its peak with full-grown and mature high school students. One may doubt Petersen's statement; in my clinical experience, the last phase of adolescence brings separation, and most often acceptance of the right of parents by the adolescents and rights of adolescents by the parents. Perhaps the term "conflict" is inappropriate for the last adolescent–parent encounter. It is rather an inevitable process of growing distance between what the parents expect and what the adolescents can accomplish in their move toward adulthood. As Blos (1979) put it, the conflict between the generations is essential for the growth of the individual and perhaps for human civilization. Some parents wish to believe that their offspring will perpetuate society and the parental sociocultural set of values (Bengtson and Troll, 1978), but many parents accept the separation.

Identification with one's peer group and becoming an "in-group" member gives the adolescent a feeling of security and power. The "we-group" makes the adolescent perceive oneself not as a child who depends on and obeys rules imposed in a heteronomous manner by the parents, but as a socionomous individual who takes part in setting the rules established by his or her peer group. Sharing of group norms means that one takes part in establishing them and willingly honors them, giving the individual the feeling of independence that leads to adult interdependence (Wolman, 1982a).

CHAPTER 5

Personality Development

ID, EGO, SUPEREGO

According to Freud, all innate drives and all that originates in the somatic organization finds its mental expression in the id. The id represents the total mental apparatus of the newborn child. The id is entirely unconscious and operates on the "pleasure principle," that is, the principle of instant gratification and impulsive behavior. The id is "a boiling cauldron of energy."

Gradually the ego and superego evolve out of the id. The ego is partly conscious and partly unconscious. The ego is the control apparatus that functions on the "reality principle." Whereas the id represents blind energy, the ego takes into consideration the potential consequences of behavior. The id pursues pleasure, come what may, but the ego seeks the most favorable and least dangerous method for obtaining pleasure. The ego acts as a watchdog, constantly testing reality; self-preservation is the ego's main task.

An inadequate development of ego leads to unpredictable and self-destructive behavior. The energies stored in the id are unbound, undirected, and uncontrolled, and may produce totally irresponsible actions.

During the first two years of life, the child faces conflict with parents in matters of toilet training. The fear of punishment and the need for affection and protection force the infant to accept the parental admonitions and to "internalize" them (i.e., to consider them his or her own).

Gradually these internalized prohibitions and self-restraints become "forerunners of the superego." Initially they are very weak and, when no one is looking, they are easily disregarded by the child. However, these "forerunners" contain the main elements of the future, namely the fear of punishment and the acceptance of parental demands as if they were the child's own. The introjected parental figures are usually idealized and seem to be more powerful and more glorious than they might be in reality. In most cases the father's image plays a greater role in the child's superego, which usually encompasses the images of both parents (Freud, 1938; Wolman, 1984a).

PERSONALITY CHANGES IN ADOLESCENCE

In the preadolescent period the superego helps the ego to maintain control over the id. Most children at this age like authoritarian teachers "who tell them what to do" and follow rigid moralistic rules.

Puberty brings about a powerful increase in instinctual demands, and the early adolescent's impulsiveness, sexual arousal, and aggressiveness bear witness to the abundance of id forces. The personality of the adolescent thus resembles a car in which the power of the engine (the id) is increased without a proportionate increase of the control apparatus of steering and braking (the ego and superego). In most instances, the decline of parental influence decreases the power of the superego in adolescence.

Not every adolescent goes through the same degree of emotional turmoil. Freud's developmental stages represent *potential* but not necessarily inevitable patterns of developmental phases. Why a particular individual remains fixated or smoothly passes from one stage to another depends on his or her genetic disposition and environmental influences (Freud, 1958).

The adolescent ego faces a multitude of new tasks. It has to establish realistic plans for the future, develop adult sexual relations, and defend itself against anxieties stemming from the growing demands of the id. Adolescents are often driven by the id, originating libido and destrudo impulses, to rush into actions they may regret later. They begin tasks or projects full of optimism and enthusiasm, only to end in quick disappointment and abandonment of their grandiose and often unrealistic plans. One day they may come forth with far-reaching plans, but the zeal may last for a short while only. The inability to maintain persistent, tenacious effort is typical of adolescents.

AN ANCIENT COMMENT

Adolescents are no longer children, nor are they what they will be in the future. Most of them are torn by inner conflicts exacerbated by a decline in parental authority. On one hand their infantile id impulses drive them to actions they may regret, and on the other hand their plans for a glorious future are often premature and unrealistic. In *Rhetoric*, Aristotle described adolescence as follows (Kiel, 1964):

The young are in character prone to desire and ready to carry any desire they may have formed into action. Of bodily desires it is the sexual to which they are most disposed to give way, and in regard to sexual desire they exercise no self-restraint. They are changeful too, and fickle in their desires, which are as transitory as they are vehement; for their wishes are keen without being permanent, like a sick man's fits of hunger and thirst. They are passionate and irascible, and apt to be carried away by their impulses. They are the slaves, too, of their passion, as their ambition prevents their ever brooking a slight . and renders them indignant at the mere idea of enduring an injury. And while they are fond of honor, they are fonder still of victory; for superiority is the object of youthful desire, and victory is a species of superiority. They regard themselves as omniscient and are positive in their assertions; this is, in fact, the reason for their carrying everything too far. Also their offenses take the line of insolence and not of meanness. They are compassionate from supposing all people to be virtuous, or at least better than they really are; for as they estimate their neighbors by their own guilelessness, they regard the evils which befall them as undeserved. Finally, they are fond of laughter and consequently facetious, facetiousness being disciplined insolence.

CHANGING MOODS

The infantile ego confuses the outside stimuli with the "inner sources of excitation." The ego of preadolescents is mature enough to refute fairy tales and to insist on fact and truth. As years go by, adolescents become more mature and have at their disposal the intellectual abilities of abstract thinking (Inhelder and Piaget, 1958). There is no question that 16-year-olds are more capable of clear thinking and of drawing logical inferences than 10-year-olds. The 10-year-olds may dream of the unknown, but adolescents can make realistic decisions concerning it.

Adolescents face important development tasks, such as accepting their own physique, their masculine or feminine role, and forming new relations with age-mates of both sexes. All adolescents crave independence and think often of their choice for a future occupation. The development of intellectual skills and concepts enables them to go ahead toward socially responsible behavior that involves preparation for a career, marriage, and family life (Lerner and Busch-Rossnagel, 1981).

The gulf between wish and reality is typical for all adolescents and results in radical mood changes. Many adolescents are in a continuous search for role models. Their attitudes change frequently, from harsh criticism of the adult society, to glorification of themselves and their idols, to severe self-criticism and feelings of helplessness and nothingness. Sometimes they believe themselves to be brilliant and glamorous, and sometimes they view themselves as physically and mentally immature creatures. Most often they are self-centered, highly concerned with their appearance and with the impression they make on others. Sometimes adolescent boys and girls believe themselves to be invulnerable, supreme beings that should attract everyone's attention and respect, and at the same time they may be painfully self-conscious and aware of true or imagined shortcomings (Blos, 1979; Erikson, 1968; Jessor, 1984; Lerner and Foch, 1987; Steinberg, 1985).

Their intellectual development enables adolescents to reexamine parental rules, and their physical and emotional growth motivates them to strike out on their own in search of their own values. Practically all adolescents ask themselves the question, "Who am I?", and in their striving toward adulthood they seek to establish a sense of personal identity. Apparently, the main theme of adolescence is the *search for identity,* and the need to know who one is, what one believes in, and what one wants to accomplish in his or her life (Erikson, 1968; Weiner, 1970; Wolman, 1984b).

At the age of 16½, in May 1796, Napoleon Bonaparte wrote:

Why am I really in the world? As I must die some time it would perhaps be better if I killed myself! If I had already sixty years behind me, I would respect the prejudices of my contemporaries and wait patiently for nature to complete her work. But, as I am beginning to feel the seriousness of life, and nothing any longer gives me pleasure, why should I suffer the days from which I can promise myself no further good? What a gap there is between mankind and nature! How cowardly, base and crawling men are! . . .

Life has become a burden to me, for I no longer enjoy any pleasure, and everything causes me pain. It is a burden to me because the people with whom I live, and probably always shall live, have manners and customs which are as different from mine as the light of the moon from that of the sun. I cannot, therefore, live as I should wish to, and thence arises an aversion to everything. (Quoted after Kircheisen, 1931, pp. 17–18)

THE SEARCH FOR MEANING

The *need* to find out who one is and what one would like to do and accomplish in life is typical of all adolescents, but how successful they are in this *search for identity* largely depends on what their *environment* has to offer them.

There is nothing in the organic nature and biological processes that indicates a goal, a purpose, or a meaning in or of human life. As long as one lives only for oneself, earning a living and defending oneself against external threats, one's life is conducted on a low biological level. "Alienation" is a colloquialism that describes aimlessness, willful isolation, and selfishness. People who care for others, who desire to have a goal in life, and who are willing to assume social responsibility are not alienated. They may disapprove of what they see around them and strive to reach higher levels, and this desire is typical for normal adolescent development. The question, "Who am I?" leads to another question: "Where is all this leading me and what is my role in life?"

The answer is gradually found through the process of identification, first with one's parents, then one's peers, and later with the society at large, or a segment of it. In late adolescence or young adulthood an individual defines himself or herself as a liberal or conservative, Catholic or Presbyterian, and so on. One's "we-ego" takes over the role of the superego (Beech and Schoeppe, 1974; Klineberg et al., 1979; Rokeach, 1979; Wolman, 1973a).

THE WE-EGO

The formation of the "we-ego" is indicative of a higher level of personality development. It implies a voluntary participation in setting norms and rules in contradiction to the superego, which is an acceptance of norms and rules *imposed* by the parents. One may point to the difference between obeying a well-meaning ruler (superego) to a democratic system of participating in and abiding by mutually-agreed-upon laws (we-ego). The superego implies obedience, the we-ego means collective responsibility. The development of the we-ego may lead to a better understanding and eventual acceptance of and participation in a democratic society. However, in some instances it may lead to the formation of antidemocratic and antisocial cliques and groups, to be described in Part II of this book. In the majority of cases, participation in a peer society and the development of the we-ego is a constructive step away from childhood dependence on one's parents toward adult interdependence and sharing of a mutually-agreed-upon system of rules and regulations.

Piaget (1965) and Kohlberg (1976) distinguished three levels of moral development, namely: (1) the *preconventional* level (ages 9–11), (2) the *conventional* level of adolescents and adults who accept social rules and regulations, and (3) the *postconventional* level of universal moral principles. I suggested a five-level system, starting with: (1) the infantile *anomous* phase, with a total lack of self-restraint and narcissistic and unlimited selfishness; (2) the childhood *phobonomous* phase of fear and defensive-aggressive behavior; (3) the late childhood *heteronomous* phase, where the child accepts the rules and regulations imposed by his or her parents; (4) the *socionomous* phase of adolescents and many adults who accept rules that they take part in establishing; and (5) the *autonomous* phase. Not all adults attain *autonomy*, which is accepting full responsibility for one's behavior and assuming a moral commitment to society as a whole (Wolman, 1982a).

It is an open question as to whether people practice what they believe in. Ajzen and Fishbein (1977) tried to explain the fact that attitudes are not always followed by action. They maintain that there are four distinct elements that determine the connection between attitude and behavior, namely: (1) the element of action, (2) the goal or the target of the action, (3) the specific context of the action, and (4) the time of the action. They believe that if one could correctly assess all the four factors, the behavior related to the attitude could be predicted.

One may or may not agree with this theory, but one may doubt its applicability to adolescent behavior. I believe Abelson (1972) was right when he wrote that the cognitive concepts of morality are practically useless in the prediction of moral behavior. I am going even further by saying that the so-called "moral principles" are meaningful only if they lead to moral behavior (Wolman, in press).

Moreover, adolescent moral values are quite unstable, and they are easily influenced by the prevailing social climate. McKinney, Hotch, and Truhon (1977) studied achievement values and moral values of adolescents. They compared the responses of adolescents in 1969 and 1975 to such questions as "I am proud of myself when . . ." and "I would be ashamed of myself if . . .". The responses given in 1969 emphasized the social-moral issues, whereas the 1975 responses stressed more personal achievement. Apparently, the prevailing social climate affects the attitudes and moral values of adolescents.

THE SEARCH FOR IDENTITY

A study of 17- to 18-year-old males and females in Denmark points out the development of the concept of self and identity. The attainment of identity was closely related to increased self-discipline and the ability to control one's own behavior. The increased self-discipline was associated with decreased dependence on one's parents. Self-assertion and the rejection of parental authority was closely related to the sense of one's own value, identity, and the planning of one's own life (Matteson, 1974).

Identification with a peer group leads to willing acceptance of rules which the member of the group participated in establishing. At the final stage of adolescence and toward adulthood, many an individual moves toward the *autonomous phase* by accepting responsibility for his or her own life. The autonomous phase implies the ability to make one's own decisions and then accept responsibility for the consequences. Autonomy means living by the rules and demands imposed by oneself on oneself, and having the courage of one's convictions. The individual moves from heteronomy, imposed by parents, through socionomy, shared by the group, to responsibility for oneself and autonomy (Wolman, 1982a).

The awareness of one's identity is closely related to one's psychosexual identity. When in late adolescence or early adulthood a male or female asks the question, "Who am I?", they have in mind "Who am I as man or as a woman?" (Money, 1980; Wolman and Money, 1980). Identification with one's own gender and acceptance of what is usually expected from that particular gender plays a highly significant role in the development of the awareness of one's self and identity.

CHAPTER 6

Psychosexual Roles

BETWEEN BIOLOGY AND SOCIOLOGY

Psychosexual identity, the awareness of being a man or a woman, is an integral and highly relevant element of the adolescent search for identity. Whatever they wish to be is closely related to their gender.

The issue of psychosexual identity must remind researchers of the discrepancy between the biological process of maturation and the attainment of psychosocial maturity. According to the so-called "secular trend" (Roche, 1979), boys and girls are sexually mature earlier than their parents, and their craving for early sexual relations is quite pronounced. However, their readiness for adult life does not keep pace with their physiological development (Adelson, 1980; Lerner and Foch, 1987; Rutter, 1980; Siegel, 1982).

In ancient societies there was practically no gulf between physiological matura-tion and social expectations. In ancient Israel, a 13-year-old boy was believed to be ready for marriage and expected to assume full responsibility for his behavior. Today's 13-year-old Jewish children can enjoy the bar mitzvah parties organized by their parents, but they are no more mature than other 13-year-olds. In many primitive societies physiological maturation led to acceptance by the adult society. Today the legal age of social maturity is 18, but 18-year-olds still need years before they are ready to accept the two main obligations of adult life, namely breadwinning and marriage and parenthood.

Contemporary civilized societies have a difficult time in coping with the gulf between biological maturation and the need for prolonged education that should prepare adolescents to join the adult society. During the necessarily long prepara-tion period, parents and society at large must guide adolescents toward their future psychosexual roles as men and women. In the past, parents stressed the sexual stereotypes and lectured their children on how to become "real men" and "real women" in the future. What they believed to be the proper psychosexual education was applied to infants, children, and adolescents following the generally accepted sexual stereotypes.

SEXUAL STEREOTYPES

In the not-too-distant past even scientists accepted and advocated the popular psychosexual stereotypes. For instance, Helene Deutsch (1945) maintained that women are narcissistic, passive, and masochistic. They do not take initiative, but tend to wait for things to happen and passively accept whatever goes on. In Freud's time, in the conservative social climate of Vienna, masculinity and femininity were described as follows:

> When you say "masculine" you mean as a rule "active," and when you say "feminine" you mean passive. . . . The male sexual cell is active and mobile; it seeks out the female one, while the latter is stationary and waits passively. This behavior of the elementary organism of sex is more or less a model of the behavior of the individuals of each sex in sexual intercourse. The male pursues the female for the purpose of sexual unity, seizes her and pushes his way into her. (Freud, 1932)

Sexual stereotypes are still widely accepted. Lerner and Shea (1982) reported several studies that stressed independence, competitiveness, and dominance in males, and affection, consideration, and compassion in females.

Cross-cultural studies prove that the sexual stereotypes are not universal, however. Margaret Mead (1949) described several sociocultural groups where the sexual stereotypes did not apply. In New Guinea, males and females of the Arapesh tribe were described by Mead as being friendly, cooperative, and considerate. Male and female children were brought up the same way, and adult men and women shared child care and household responsibilities. Likewise, Mead did not find significant behavioral differences between males and females of the Mundugumor tribe. Aggressive, belligerent behavior was common to both males and females, and both were hostile to their children. Finally, the Tschambuli tribesmen presented what could be regarded by American standards as a reversal of social roles. The women displayed more initiative and more businesslike manners than the men.

Many of the so-called masculine and feminine traits are culturally imposed. Some American Indians expected fearless behavior in boys. Little boys who failed to conform and who displayed weakness and admitted fear or pain were ostracized and forced to join the subservient female gender. They were treated like transvestites and forced to do women's work.

Munroe, Munroe, and Whiting (1981) followed the gender difference issues in their cross-cultural studies as well. They reported that in the Polynesian culture, there are quite modest sex-role differences between males and females.

Additional cross-cultural studies did not offer much support to the idea that self-image in adolescence is the same for all members of one gender, and there are general and significant differences between the genders (Ostrov, Offer, and Howard, 1986). Obviously then, there is very little, if any, evidence in support of the sexual stereotypes. It might be useful to notice that at the present time there is little significant scientific literature describing male psychology, while numerous volumes have been written about the psychology of women. Men seem to differ from one another, and their common gender cannot obliterate the differences in intelligence, emotionality, special talents, social attitudes, and so on. No psychologist or psychiatrist believes that all men share common psychological traits and act alike just because of their gender.

The same should apply to women. The gentle and brilliant Madame Marie Curie and the Auschwitz monster Else Koch were females. The Russian Empress Catherine the Second had more in common with Tsar Ivan the Terrible than with Eleanor Roosevelt. What, then, is the origin of the idea that women are more emotional, more subtle, more fragile than men? That all men are industrious and brave, and women are cowardly and passive.

TRADITIONAL CONCEPTS

Sexual socialization, that is, accepting one's psychosexual role, is related to biological sexual maturation, for the anatomical differences between the genders are the basis for gender identity. The psychosocial gender identity is acquired through a learning process guided by parents or parental substitutes who bring up a child as a boy or as a girl. Usually this process starts about the middle of the second year of life and is firmly established before school age in 4- to 6-year-olds.

Many behavioral patterns of boys and girls represent the stereotypes of past generations that encouraged the qualities of initiative and self-assertion in boys and discouraged them in girls. Shy boys were called "sissies" and assertive girls were called "tomboys." Once a colleague of mine who was a psychiatrist brought his 14 ½-year-old son to my office. The boy attended a private school in New York City. The school psychologist recommended psychotherapy for the boy, who was spending "too much time in the school laboratory, not enough time in sports, and disliked football." The boy explained to me that he hated violence and brutal behavior, but loved science. He planned to major in chemistry and become a research scientist. He was not "alienated" or "asocial," as the school psychologist intimated, but he was not exceedingly gregarious. He had a few friends, a girlfriend, and was an excellent student. I did not find anything abnormal about the boy; I explained to the father and to the school psychologist that not everyone is extroverted, and the boy's behavior was not psychopathology.

Some traditional differences in social roles ascribed to males and females have their roots in economic life. In ancient times a male child was a blessing for parents who needed his help in plowing the fields and minding the herds. Polygamy was an economic necessity, and the more childbearing wives one had, the safer was his future. Small wonder that the Israelite forefathers cherished the Lord's blessing and his promise of "having as many children as stars in the sky and as sand on the seashore." When the Romans had abundant slave labor, children ceased to be a desired commodity.

Past ideas die slowly. For millennia men brainwashed women and wished them to be passive, submissive, and subservient. Men wished to be perceived as powerful, self-confident, self-assertive, and definitely more logical and more intelligent than women, and many obsolete and antiquated stereotypes still persist.

THE ORIGIN OF STEREOTYPES

Some of the so-called "feminine traits" originated in the socioeconomic structure of the past. A woman's task was to produce babies and take care of them; a man's task was to hunt, fish, fight, work, and provide food and protection. Motherly love and care were praised as feminine traits, courage and cunning as male traits. Women needed no initiative. While staying home, women were expected to mind the hearth, cook meals, and keep the house clean. Men were supposed to fight hostile neighbors and beasts and be brave and aggressive. Men were expected to fertilize several women; thus, they were expected to be sexually aggressive. Women were supposed to attract male sperm; thus, they were expected to be sweet, charming, and subservient. Women kept by men, whether in or outside of marriage, have received all the benefits as long as men cared about them. Small wonder that a woman was taught "to lie to men, to scheme, to be wily. In speaking to them she wears an artificial expression on her face; she is cautious, hypocritical, play-acting" (De Beauvoir, 1953).

Women had no choice but to accept their passive, subservient countenance of charming girls, subservient wives, and caring mothers; they were brainwashed to accept their social role.

"Penis envy" was a symbolic expression of rebellion of adolescent girls. The penis was envied not as a sexual organ, but as a symbol of freedom. In Freud's time many girls wished they were boys, for this was the only, though imaginary, way of escaping discrimination and subservience. Young men could go wherever they pleased, talk to whoever they wished, and choose the occupation they liked, but a girl was her father's slave until he agreed to transfer her to her future husband (Wolman, 1978b).

CHANGING VALUES

In the United States, the majority of business executives, dentists, farmers, and truck drivers are men, and the majority of nurses, secretaries, and librarians are women. All of these allegedly "natural" differences do not hold much water. In America most teachers are women and most physicians are men. In several other countries, however, most teachers are men, and in the Russian Republic most physicians are women. Today in the United States many civil leaders, government officials, and lawyers are women. No one is concerned with anatomy when choosing a dentist, a real estate broker, a restaurant server, or anyone in any other occupation. Job competence, self-confidence, and dependability are not related to one's gender and are not exclusive masculine traits.

CURRENT RESEARCH

Contemporary studies of differences between the sexes raise again the crucial issue of this present book: nature versus nurture, biological determinants versus sociopsychological issues. Current research tries to find out whether there are significant differences between males and females and what these differences are. The review of cross-cultural research points to certain behavioral differences between males and females, but it is still an open question to what extent these differences are biologically determined, or if they are a product of environmental influences (Ember, 1981). Apparently the issue is still unresolved, and whereas there is some decline in the popularity of sexual stereotypes, there is no conclusive evidence concerning the psychological differences between males and females, nor is there adequate proof as to what these differences are and whether their origin is biological or sociocultural (Segall, 1986). For instance, Goldstein and Segall (1983) reported that everywhere the most aggressive acts are performed by male adolescents, but most probably male adolescent aggressiveness is a product or combination of biological and sociocultural factors, and it is still debated which factor is more important (Dreyer, 1982).

There is also no evidence that females are more vulnerable to stress than males (Kessler and McLeod, 1985). The fact that women have a higher rate of reporting severe stress and of first admission to mental hospitals is probably related to the fact that women are more exposed to stressful situations because of their role in taking care of the family. The fact that there is a growing incidence of adolescent pregnancy contributes to greater mental health risks for adolescent girls.

In regard to self-assertion, contemporary research contradicts the early stereotypes of males being active and females being passive (Carson, 1989). Some researchers have drawn a distinction between "high-power" women who pursue careers and are well off, and the rather passive "low-power" women. High-power females compete with high-power males and look for leadership positions in many fields, whereas the non-ambitious, low-power females tend to accept more subservient positions (Winter and Stewart, 1978). The distinction between ambitious, power-craving girls and low-power, unmotivated girls is also visible in adolescent peer groups. In many instances females have been inclined to attribute their achievements not to their own abilities and efforts but rather to circumstances, whereas males tend to ascribe success to themselves (Gaeddert, 1987). In another study conducted on close to 2,000 high school students of both genders, the girls seem to have been more ambitious than the boys. Most probably the contemporary changes in social climate and in the male–female social roles have a definite, significant impact on the motivation of adolescent boys and girls in terms of career and achievement (Farmer, 1985).

THE "SEXUAL REVOLUTION"

In early adolescence sexual behavior used to be masturbation, mutual masturbation with an adolescent of the same gender, and touching, petting, and necking with an adolescent of the opposite sex. Exploration of sexy books and magazines, watching pornographic films and television, exciting conversations with peers, and using obscene language are favorite activities. The 1960s and 1970s witnessed the so-called "sexual revolution" with a considerable, almost general decline in self-inhibition and an increase in unrestrained sexual behavior of both adults and adolescents. Also, the new developments in contraceptive methods, especially the birth control pill, played a significant role in the sexual revolution (Diepold and Young, 1979).

In the 1960s, 1970s, and early 1980s, the "secular trend," as well as the new permissive attitude of the adult society, contributed to a sharp increase in the incidence of sexual intercourse in adolescence (Roche, 1979). Probably being a member of a low socioeconomic status group, belonging to an ethnic minority group, and the widespread use of alcohol and drugs (to be discussed in Part II of this book) are to be counted as additional causes of increased sexual relations in adolescence. For boys, sexual freedom is often related to self-assertion, rebellion against traditional values, and, in some instances, the influence of alcohol and drugs. Liberated and independent girls actively pursue sexual activity, but even more traditional adolescent females often engage in sex in pursuit of their identity. Quite often they gain self-respect by associating with older sexual partners (Chilman, 1983; Dreyer, 1982).

SEXUAL BEHAVIOR

According to the "secular trend" (Roche, 1979), at the present time adolescents are physiologically ready for sexual intercourse at an earlier age than their parents, and much earlier than their grandparents. In the Kinsey reports of 1948 and 1953, 68 percent of boys and 84 percent of girls 15 years old had reached orgasm by masturbation. Only 24 percent of males and 3 percent of females experienced coitus by the age of 15.

According to Zelnick and Kantner (1977), of 15-year-old girls who had experienced coitus, 38.4 percent were black and 13.8 percent were white. The differences were basically the same when related to the socioeconomic differences;

apparently lower socioeconomic status is related to early sexual behavior: Of 19-year-old girls who had sexual intercourse, 83.7 percent were black and 48.7 percent were white. About 40 percent of males had their first intercourse at the age of 15 (Siegel, 1982). The poor use of contraceptives contributed to a high increase of adolescent pregnancies, births, abortions, and venereal diseases (Zelnick and Kantner, 1977).

The 1960s and 1970s brought significant changes in the sexual behavior of adolescents. At the present time, it is apparent that:

> The role and the meaning of sex in the development of adolescents has undergone a dramatic shift. . . . In the past, genital sex and sexual intercourse were considered taboo for unmarried adolescents. . . . The current evidence indicates that sex for unmarried adolescents is no longer taboo and that sexual intimacy is an important part of the identity formation process. (Dreyer, 1982, p. 595)

And further on:

> The consequences of this change in adolescent sexual behavior have been adverse in that sexually transmitted diseases, particularly gonorrhea, have become much more prevalent, and the rates of teenage pregnancy, abortions, and illegitimacy have risen sharply, especially among young teenagers in the 13 to 17 age group. However, there is very little evidence to support the notion that engaging in sexual intercourse presents serious personal or emotional problems for adolescents who use contraceptives consistently and correctly. (Dreyer, 1982, p. 596)

The 1980s have brought about the epidemic spread of acquired immunodeficiency syndrome (AIDS), a lethal disease spread by sexual relations. Most probably this will spell the end of the "sexual revolution," but the current statistical data needs a thorough evaluation.

SEX AND INTIMACY

Many adolescents face the conflict between the physical need for sex and the emotional need for affection and loyalty. The younger ones choose the physical aspects ahead of the emotional aspects of sexuality, whereas as they get older they may cherish intimacy and emotional ties in sexual relations (Reis and Shaver, 1989).

In primitive cultures, and in some individuals in civilized societies, the physical aspects prevail and emotional ties do not always develop or develop only gradually. Civilized societies usually advocate some degree of self-restraint and wish to see sexual relations as the intimate end-product of love, affection, and courtship. Civilized societies differ in regard to the degree of their norms, preferences, controls, and prohibitions, but practically all of them endeavor to enhance the emotional aspects of sexual relations (Money, 1980; Wolman and Money, 1980).

Lower-socioeconomic-class adolescents usually have fewer inhibitions and tend to start sexual intercourse earlier than those of the upper classes. This phenomenon could possibly be linked to earlier maturation of adolescents in lower socioeconomic classes. A 17- or 18-year-old sales girl or construction worker is an adult member of his or her occupation, engaged in active support of their families. They are, sociologically speaking, adults, and they may conduct their personal lives in accordance with the accepted norms and beliefs of their social class. In most instances they perceive life more realistically than their age-mate college freshmen or sophomores. Despite Karl Marx's prophecy, the working-class youth tend to be less revolutionary and less rebellious than their affluent college age-mates. Moreover, working youth are more inclined to accept the existing cultural norms and assume the responsibilities of marriage and family earlier. In many instances they will marry their premarital sexual partner (Dreyer, 1982).

And here is the paradox. In the 1960s and 1970s, middle- and upper-class adolescents started to act as free sexually as their lower-class age-mates. Sexual intercourse is presently as commonly practiced in private high schools and Ivy League colleges as in the streetcorner society. Today, one can hardly find a 19-year-old who has not had sexual intercourse.

One may counterpose two patterns of sexual behavior, the one that proceeds from physical to emotional and the other from emotional to physical. The first seems to be more primitive and the second more refined. In the United States today, the more primitive pattern is practiced among younger and less-educated adolescents, who eventually may outgrow this pattern and become affectionate husbands and wives and responsible parents (Money, 1980; Siegel, 1982).

On lower levels of biological evolution sex is sheer physiology, but in a certain species when two fish stay together after copulation the psychosocial element is added to physiology. Sexually involved fish usually hunt together for food, protect one another, and share social status within the "pecking order"; their interaction is more than sex; for all practical purposes they are "married." Also, when male wolves hunt for food for the female and their cubs, they have formed families.

Psychosocial maturity in sex implies the ability to choose a sexual partner and develop a satisfactory and lasting relationship with him or her, and then provide adequate care for the offspring. Thus, early adolescents can be biosexually mature, but psychosexually they are immature.

Early adolescents frequently become attracted to the opposite sex, but their choices are unstable, haphazard, and often self-contradictory. Early adolescent boys and girls dream of never ending conquests, but they are unable to retain any of them. They are often unhappy about their present and past choices and perpetually dream about future and greener pastures. It takes years before they realize that one cannot have everything and that numerous transient relations may leave them dissatisfied (Chilman, 1983; Dreyer, 1982).

One of the major tasks in adolescent behavior is the integration of the sexual urge with an interpersonal relationship. Being physically attracted to and loving someone are two different things that may or may not be related. In early adolescent boys the two are usually far apart; sometimes a boy adores a "nice girl" whom he wouldn't dare to touch and practices sex with a girl for whom he has no respect whatsoever. In girls the desire to form a meaningful relationship may start earlier than sexual craving (Deaux and Major, 1987).

Mature individuals are capable of making a rational and lasting choice as to who they would like to share their lives with. A combination of physical attraction, genuine friendship, and psychological maturity on the part of both partners is a solid foundation for a successful marriage.

PSYCHOSEXUAL ROLES

The male psychosexual role was often related to a particular role men were supposed to play in their respective societies. In ancient Sparta, young men who belonged to the ruling class were given heavy armor at the age of 20. The heavier the armor, the greater the distinction, for the main task of the men in Sparta was to fight enemies and come home from a war "either with a shield or on a shield." Many primitive tribes stressed endurance, courage, and perseverance in male puberty rites, for those were the traits necessary for the survival of the tribe. The readiness to earn a living and assume responsibility for the family has been the essence of puberty rites even in primitive societies (Adelson, 1980; Kandel and Lesser, 1972; Mead, 1949; Rutter, 1980; Steinberg, 1985).

It is therefore a fallacy to relate adulthood to sexual practices. The main connection between sex and adulthood is socioeconomic responsibility; children can practice sex in this way or another, and adolescents can produce children, but adults assume *responsibility* for their offspring. Most boys and girls can practice sex before they reach the midpoint of their teens, but as long as they cannot support themselves and their offspring, they are not yet adults.

At the present time the gender differences could be described as differences in sexual functions, reproduction, and certain aspects of child care. The fact is that only women menstruate, gestate (carry children), and lactate (breast feed). Only men can get erections, insert penises, and fertilize. At a certain age women undergo menopause and cannot become pregnant; they may, however, continue sexual relations. Old men can fertilize women, but the sexual drive and sexual performance gradually deteriorate with advanced age (Wolman, 1978b).

SEXUALITY EDUCATION

"Sexuality education" is a much broader term than "sex education." Sex education was usually limited to physical aspects of social behavior with an emphasis on preventing pregnancy and venereal diseases. In 1979 a conference of concerned experts in Uppsala, Sweden suggested broad outlines for "sexuality education." The proposed principles included accurate information about sexual behavior combined with several psychological issues, such as equality of males and females, responsibility in sexual behavior, and integrating sex with overall life planning and adult human relations.

Sexuality education should help adolescents to treat sexual behavior as an integral part of personality development. Petting and coitus without emotional involvement can be experienced as purely mechanical or even exploitive behavior. If it goes on for years, it may reduce one's ability for a deep emotional attachment and adversely affect one's personality growth. Purely physical sexuality may impoverish one's life experiences and foster a cold, calculated, mechanical attitude to people of the opposite sex. In some instances, sex without affection breeds selfish, uncaring behavior typical of exploitive sociopaths and violent rapists.

Sexuality education should encourage *responsible behavior*. It should give precise and adequate information related to the anatomy and physiology of sex and of the reproductive process, but this is not enough. Mature sexual behavior is an *interactional process* in which two people take part. It should include more than physiology; it must be an important and complex process that involves affection, consideration and care, and preparation for parenthood, the most responsible commitment to a human life which the parents create.

Animals copulate; human beings make love. One can live one's life on a low, animalistic level, but one can enhance and enrich one's experience by investing emotional attachment, care, and loyalty. Sex can be practiced by masturbation; sex can be practiced for a fee in a brothel; sex can be abuse and rape. But sex can be a meaningful experience of two human beings in love. Sex is also the only road toward parenthood and to giving love to one's children (Wolman and Money, 1980).

Some time ago I had in psychotherapy a young married couple. Paul was a college professor and Mary was a busy newspaper reporter. Paul complained that Mary neglected her household duties. Mary explained that Paul taught twelve to fifteen hours a week and possibly spent fifteen hours in research and classroom preparations, whereas she was spending at least forty hours a week on her job and often much more. I suggested that they hire a housekeeper, but both of them preferred not to spend the money. My alternative proposal was as follows: "Please hire a housekeeper. On Monday, Wednesday, and Friday her name is Mary. On Tuesday, Thursday, and Saturday her name is Paul. On Sundays she will be off." My suggestion was accepted, successfully implemented, and contributed to a harmonious relationship.

Sexuality education could help boys and girls to become mature men and women, willing to share adult responsibilities as husbands, fathers, wives, and mothers.

CHAPTER 7

Toward
Self-Supporting Behavior

There are three distinct phases in adolescent adjustment: in *early* adolescence the
rapid *physical* growth and bodily changes present the main challenge. In *middle*
adolescence the striving for independence from parents and developing a network
of social relations with peers of the same and of the opposite gender are the chief
issue. In *late* adolescence the search for identity and planning for the future domi-
nate the picture. It has to be added at this point that the problems of an early phase
do not disappear; the new problems grow on top of the old ones (Erikson, 1968;
Offer and Offer, 1975; Siegel, 1982; Van Hasselt and Hersen, 1987).

The transition from adolescence to adulthood is characterized by an increasing
concern with what the future has in store and a progressively realistic approach to
vocational choice. Adolescents give up the childish dreams of becoming a police-
man and a surgeon and a fireman and a pilot, all at the same time, and they begin to
seriously think of their future vocational role. Their vocational planning is usually
related to a variety of factors, such as parental occupation, peer influence, social
class, and their own interests, inclinations, and abilities. Quite often they overestimate or underestimate their ability, and their vocational choice is not always conducive to a successful vocational role in the future.

Following the life-span approach, Super (1984) explained the role of the various
factors that determine one's vocational life. Super used the term "theater" when he
described the roles of home, community, school, and workplace of one's career.
These "theaters" determine the "roles" people play. Further on, Super describes
life-span roles, namely child, student, homemaker. These roles interact with the
five life phases of growth, exploration, establishment, maintenance, and decline.

Age is a very important determinant in the role one plays as a child, adolescent, or adult. Adolescents face the task of choosing and planning their future career. In adolescence occupation preferences are closely related to what adolescents think of themselves and what they believe they will be able to attain in the future.

Farmer (1985) tested 2,000 high school boys and girls and found that adolescents' vocational aspirations depend on their personality makeup, but also depend considerably on environmental influences. According to Farmer, high school girls have higher career aspirations than boys. It is probable that the recent women's liberation trend inspires adolescent females to move ahead in life, whereas adolescent males have lost some of their hoped-for superiority (Nesselrode and Baltes, 1979; Rutter, 1980).

CHANGE OF OCCUPATION

The development toward realistic occupational choice can be divided into the three following periods:

1. The *fantasy* period, from the age of 5 to the beginning of adolescence, when everything seems possible.

2. The *tentative choice* period, from about 12 to 16 or 17. At this period peer influences are of great importance and many adolescents make tentative choices, following their peers with some consideration of their own intellectual or artistic interests, but with little consideration of realistic possibilities and practical aspects of their planned careers.

3. The period of *realistic choice* may start as early as the age of 16 or 17, but it may also be delayed for several years (Adelson, 1980; Super, 1984; Vondracek and Lerner, 1982).

There are four objective criteria for a rational choice of occupation, namely aptitude, interests, practical aspects, and overall personality consideration. I had in psychotherapy a young man who decided to become a virtuoso violinist despite his late start in playing the violin and rather mediocre abilities. The desire to be successful in one's career is universal and perfectly rational, but success greatly depends on one's abilities and is not a matter of wishful thinking. Awareness of one's potentialities is a prerequisite of rational choice.

Moreover, people spend most of their waking hours on their jobs, and it is rather difficult to be successful doing something one dislikes. No occupation is a joy-ride, but a basic inclination and a considerable degree of interest is the second criterion for vocational choice.

Practical economic considerations are the third criterion of vocational choice. People live off their jobs, and one's choice of occupation must take into account the need to earn a living.

Overall personality aspects and the way one views oneself are the last but not least criterion of vocational choice. One spends his or her lifetime in a certain occupation and interacts with other people in the same field. Friends and relatives, strangers and neighbors relate to him or her as the dentist or shopkeeper, electrician or stockbroker, cabinet maker or mailman. One interacts daily with a certain group of people, and one's social life is considerably influenced by one's occupation. Moreover, one must accept one's occupation as a major avenue for one's abilities and interests and identify oneself with the vocational role throughout one's adult life.

VOCATIONAL GUIDANCE

Adolescents need vocational guidance that should make them aware of their potentialities and limitations. Most vocational guidance programs in the public school systems emphasize self-knowledge and learning as the basis for decision-making. In junior high school they stress exploration of vocational options and preliminary planning, and in senior high school they foster specific planning and initial implementation of vocational decisions (Holland, 1985).

A longitudinal study of high school students (Vondracek and Lerner, 1982) pointed to the following seven points indicative of vocational maturity:

1. *Crystallization of interest*, that is, consistency of vocational preferences and the presence of a primary interest pattern.

2. *Appropriateness of preferences*, that is, whether the vocational choice is related to abilities and interests as well as to socioeconomic forces.

3. *Work experience*, related to summer and vacation work experience.

4. *Occupational information*, that is, what the student knows about the occupation he or she would like to choose.

5. *Acceptance of responsibility* in choosing an occupation and undergoing the necessary training.

6. *Planning*.

7. *Implementation*.

MALE AND FEMALE VOCATIONAL ROLES

Vocational and family roles of men and women are undergoing significant changes. The vast majority of American couples have children, but with the increase of women's participation in the labor force there has been a decrease in birth rate. During the last twenty-five years the birth rate in the United States dropped almost 50 percent, and the two-children family is becoming an almost general norm.

The traditional role of wife and mother is no longer satisfactory for a majority of American women. Contemporary women aspire to equal rights in marriage and in economic, cultural, and political life. Most women combine their marital and parental obligations with the pursuit of an active career life. Men begin to share household and parental duties, which eventually put an end to the traditional concepts of the "active" masculine and "passive" feminine life.

In 1900 only 5.5 percent of married women were employed, in the 1980s about 50 percent. In the 1960s 37.7 percent of women over the age of 16 were gainfully employed, and in the 1980s 58 percent of women over 16 were gainfully employed. In the 1960s about one-half of American families had one breadwinner, while in the 1980s over two-thirds of American families had two breadwinners, and both husband and wife were gainfully employed (Astin, 1985).

As a rule, employed women are more satisfied with their lives than housewives. Middle-aged married career women have higher self-esteem than housewives and feel that they are better mothers. Apparently, a combination of family and occupational life is more satisfactory to women than just a family or just an occupation.

According to Fassinger (1985), who studied the vocational attitudes of female college students, female students' aptitude, their self-attitude, the spirit of women's liberation, and their craving for achievement greatly influence their choice of career. The ratios of girls who choose traditionally masculine vocational roles grows rapidly, and more and more young adults of both genders plan to share family responsibilities with breadwinning employment (Farmer, 1983; Vondracek and Lerner, 1982; Walsh and Osipow, 1986).

CHAPTER 8

Socialization
and Self-Determination

THREE TYPES OF SOCIAL RELATIONS

In a society based on freedom of association, people can choose to belong to various groups and organizations. As adolescents grow up they may increase their social participation by marriage, by getting a job, by moving into a new neighborhood, or by making new friends. As years go by they may relinquish former associations, forget their schoolmates, renounce their religious or political affiliations, and sever their relationships with parents and other family members (Adelson, 1980; Datan and Reese, 1977; Klineberg et al., 1979; Offer and Offer, 1975).

Let's elaborate on the division of social relations briefly described in Chapter 3. One can divide friendly social relations according to the aims of the participants, depending on whether their main purpose is the satisfaction of their own needs (*instrumental*), their partners' (*vectorial*), or both (*mutual* or *mutual acceptance*) (Wolman, 1974).

People may join others in order to have their own needs satisfied; they have in mind to *take* and *not give*. In such a case the individual considers others as tools or instruments. He joins others because without them he could not satisfy his needs or would encounter considerable difficulties. Whenever the particular relationship or the particular group ceases to satisfy his needs, he will leave it.

This kind of relationship is called *instrumental*, and is typical in business relationships. When a man or a woman looks for a job, they enter an instrumental social relationship and their objective is to *receive* a salary. The employer's attitude is instrumental also, for the only thing he or she wants is to find someone to *help him or her* in their trade. When a student registers for a course, his or her attitude is also instrumental, for they want to receive knowledge or a degree.

Under favorable conditions the growing child gradually develops and learns consideration for other people. Childhood friendship relationships signal a beginning of the *mutual* or *mutual acceptance* relationship that eventually reaches the peak in adolescence. In adolescent friendship both partners are willing to give the emotion they experience, which can be called friendship, consideration, or love; they are willing to renounce some of their benefits for the sake of their partner; they are willing to protect their partner and to make him or her happy. It is the beginning of voluntary giving (Flavell and Markman, 1983). Adolescents insist on mutuality. Each partner is willing to give and expects the other partner to feel the same way (Feather, 1980; Money, 1980).

In a mutual relationship, *the aim is to give and to receive*. Hence there is *love* in them, love being defined as willingness to care and to help. In instrumental relationships there is the desire to receive love but not to give it. In mutual relations there is the desire to give and to receive.

Parenthood is the prototype of *vectorialism*. Parents create life, protect it, and care for it irrespective of their child's looks, health, IQ, disposition, and success. No human being can be vectorial all the time. Some human beings never develop vectorial attitudes, whereas others develop them frequently and to a great extent.

Normally, human beings are capable of functioning adequately in all three types of social relations. They are instrumental in business, mutual in marriage, and vectorial in parenthood. There has never been a 100 percent vectorial society. Most often a complex social structure includes all three elements, and its members are instrumental in breadwinning activities, mutual in marriage, and vectorial in regard to their children. However, when the society as a whole is in danger many individuals rally to the defense of all in idealistic, self-sacrificing, and vectorial behavior (Wolman, 1973a, 1984b).

This vectorialism is often fostered through educational means, taught by parents and teachers, reinforced by tradition and religion, and glorified in art and literature. The realistic and practical Romans told about Mucius Scaevola, who put his hand on fire; the Swiss tell stories of heroism with regard to Wilhelm Tell and Winkelried.

EDUCATION FOR SOCIAL RESPONSIBILITIES

Adolescents do not live in a vacuum, nor are they original creators of new ideas. Even when they rebel against traditional values, the rebellion is inspired by some social forces acting within the adult society, such as religion, communism, fascism, nationalism, or some other "ism" or anti-"ism." Adolescent groups tend to conform to those adult forces that promise *immediate participation in decision-making processes of the adult society* (Rokeach, 1979; Rutter, 1980).

Bronfenbrenner (1970) compared the impact of adult society and of peers on adolescents in the United States and the former Soviet Union. He found that adult pressure in both societies reduces the "in-group" solidarity of peer groups. However, as far as peer pressure is concerned, in the United States it increases deviation from the norms and standards of the adult society, while in the former Soviet Union it reinforced behavioral patterns approved by the adult society. When the adult society renounces its responsibility toward its adolescents and blocks their progress to adulthood, adolescents may form regressive groupings where preadolescent values such as being tough, arrogant, and mischievous prevail. Whenever the adolescent stirring for adulthood is thwarted, the tendency to form antisocial gangs increases, but whenever adolescents are encouraged to participate in the adult society and partake in performing valuable services for the society, their tendency for forming antisocial groups disappears.

> For example, the voluntary labor contribution of young Yugoslavs in road building has resulted in a youth movement dedicated to national development—concrete evidence of youth's participation, involvement, and importance.
> The same theme is put forth for the Pioneers and the Komsomol youth groups in the Soviet Union. Here the political involvement is very pronounced, but the underlying message of youth's importance and youth's anticipated contribution to the national cause are stressed and magnified, never underestimated or minimized. When the activities of these youth groups are compared with the programs of the YMCA, Boy Scouts and Girl Scouts, or the CYO, the American groups are differentiated by the fact that their energy investment is directed more to play than to work and the focus of activity is more often upon egocentric rather than on sociocivic goals. (Bronfenbrenner, 1970)

In the Israeli collective settlements (kibbutz), strong peer bonds are created. As the children grow, they go through transitions from one child's house to another and from one set of school/work experiences to another. The kibbutz adolescents develop a sense of belonging and membership in a large family. There is strong pressure toward conformity among adolescent peers, and one of the strongest motives for continuing one's commitment to the kibbutz community is the sense of obligation and love for one's peers. The group inspires its members to reject the selfish attitudes and potential luxury of noncommunal life for the security and moral values of the kibbutz (Rabin, 1983).

THE SEARCH FOR SPIRITUAL VALUES

Many late adolescents can and wish to be motivated by a high degree of idealism. This idealism can reveal itself in a variety of ways depending on the individual and his or her environment. Even today, despite the present social climate of disinhibition, there are a great many deeply religious adolescents (Wolman, 1983). Late adolescents on the verge of young adulthood tend to become less dogmatic and less rigid in their political and religious convictions. In many instances their previous

religious and political beliefs are questioned, modified, changed, and even aban-
doned. Some adolescents may, however, become more involved in religion and
mysticism, seeking answers to the problems of society, ethics, and the universe.
They may join one of the religious sects or embrace Zen Buddhism or develop
their own individualistic, highly speculative religious or semi-religious concepts
(Beech and Schoeppe, 1974; Biner, 1987).

Though the impact of organized religion has considerably weakened, the search
for the ultimate truth leads many adolescents back into the religious community,
which may or may not find a way to convey its moral principles to the younger
generation (Adelson, 1980; Rokeach, 1979).

Apparently, American adolescents are hungry for moral values and are in dire
need of spiritual guidance. Thus, whereas many adolescents defect from Catholic,
Protestant, and Jewish religions, many join the more outspoken and extreme conservative groups. Some fundamentalist and traditionalist groups have attracted many
adolescents, among them the Navigators and Campus Crusade for Christ and Jewish Orthodox groups.

The fact that so many adolescents join the various cults serves as additional
proof that they are hungry for spiritual values. Some of the cults are pathological or
even criminal and exploit the enthusiasm of their naive followers. The young men
and women who join cults want to devote themselves to a worthy cause and, faced
by inadequate guidance and unresponsive adults, follow dubious slogans and often
fall prey to dishonest cult leaders.

Apparently the *need* to believe might be stronger than the belief itself. Many
adolescents have lost faith in their parents and, by the same token, in the adult
society, and are looking for an objective and stable set of values. When they rebel
against their parents, whether they turn to cults or any other religious or political
group, they do believe that their lives have become meaningful and they are serving a noble purpose (Wolman, 1973b).

SELF-DETERMINATION

Adolescents seek the answers to the questions, "Who am I?" and "What is the
meaning of my life?" They are usually unaware of the fact that there is no particular
point in life when one's identity is established. Identity is a dynamic and not a static
concept, and the search for identity does not come to a happy conclusion with the
end of adolescence. As long as one lives one reevaluates one's identity in relationship to one's family life and vocational career, and to the society one belongs to as
a whole. The search for solutions to old and new problems goes on, but the end of
adolescence should augur a more realistic, more sober, and more responsible attitude toward oneself and to whoever one interacts with. The decisions and life choices
of young adults should come from within, related to their set of values (Beech and
Schoeppe, 1974; Erikson, 1968; Hogan and Emier, 1978; Kohlberg, 1976).

No one lives in a vacuum, and interaction with other individuals and an active participation in contemporary cultural and political issues is related to one's set of values. The question, "Who am I?" cannot be answered outside the context of sharing and belonging. Identity does not mean isolation or alienation; it means assuming responsibility, sharing life experiences with one's family and friends, and taking part in society at large (Taifel and Turner, 1986; Van Hasselt and Hersen, 1987).

Most late adolescents outgrow their peer group dependence and the need to admire an imaginary savior. As the emotional imbalance subsides and more realistic outlooks develop, the postadolescents enter a period of productive young adulthood. In most cases the transition from adolescence to adulthood leads to positive socialization and self-determination. Many young men and women rediscover the values of their parents and of the adult society at large, and most of them join the existing occupations, enter lasting marital relationships, and become loyal members of the adult society.

Childhood means dependence on one's parents, teachers, and other adults. Adolescents rebel against dependence and wish to be independent. As they enter adulthood, they learn that adults are interdependent and that no one can singlehandedly meet his or her economic, cultural, political, and psychological needs. However, the search for meaning and identity goes on for years to come and does not come to an end with the end of adolescence.

CHAPTER 9

The Need for Guidance

PARENTAL GUIDANCE

Adolescents seem to believe that adulthood is a sort of "freedom paradise." Many adolescents believe that adults can do whatever they wish, enjoy and indulge every whim, and deny any personal liberty to their adolescent sons and daughters.

"My father does as he pleases," a 16-year-old boy asserted. "Of course, he works, but no one can force him to show up at his job. He may change his job if he wants to; anyway, nobody bosses him around the way he bosses me. On weekends and holidays he does whatever he pleases, goes fishing or hiking, takes us on a trip or leaves us home. Why can't I have the same freedom?"

Many parents do not counteract this illusion of adult freedom. They fail to explain to their sons and daughters that, as parents, they *must* work, *must* support their children, *must* pay rent or mortgage, and *must* pay taxes. Many parents ignore the ongoing technological, socioeconomic, and psychological change and offer very little, if any, guidance (Adams, 1979; Anthony, 1979; Grotevant and Cooper, 1983).

Ambivalent thoughts and feelings are one of the chief characteristics of adolescents. At one moment they are full of love and at another moment they are full of hatred. They are self-confident and insecure, hyperoptimistic and hyperpessimistic; full of enthusiasm and bursting energy one moment, and then wallowing in helpless depression the next. Adolescence has often been described as a risk-taking period, and many adolescents take chances experimenting with sex, alcohol, and drugs, often as a cover-up for feelings of inadequacy and inferiority.

THE ACCEPTING PARENTS

It is not easy to offer friendly assistance and guidance to someone who is unstable, ambivalent, and shows very little, if any, gratitude. Adolescents need a helping hand, perhaps more than younger children. They crave love and attention, and tend to reject both (Fleck, 1983).

Adolescent boys and girls are torn by doubts concerning their appearance and their intellectual abilities. They are upset by the ups and downs of their self-confidence, their bursting impulses, their difficulty in controlling them, and, above all, they are perplexed in their search for a path in life. One of the main problems of adolescents is their quest for identity, which can be perceived as a struggle for independence from parents and teachers; yet in this quest they need plenty of moral support and guidance from those very people (Hogan and Emler, 1978).

Adolescents rebel and break away from parental authority and possessiveness, but they need help in the transition from childlike dependence and adolescent rebelliousness toward adult interdependence and responsible interaction with other people. Parents who relate to their adolescent sons and daughters with tact and understanding, and share with them the rights and responsibilities of family life, plant the seeds for wholesome development. No one can learn to swim without water, and growing into adulthood is greatly helped by taking part in adult life. Maturity means responsibility, and mature parents encourage their adolescent sons and daughters in sharing responsibilities at home and outside the home (Bengtson and Troll, 1978).

Adolescents appreciate it when adults trust them and treat them respectfully. When a father asks his son to take over or partake in adult responsibilities, he helps him grow into adulthood. But when parents either overtly reject them or, ridden by guilt feelings, bribe or overprotect them, adolescents lose faith in their parents and don't rely on them any longer. Adolescents who have friendly and understanding parents tend to develop better relationships with their peers, teachers, and other adults, and show more self-confidence in their outlook on life. Adolescents who feel accepted by their parents are better prepared for their future marital and parental roles than those who believe their parents reject them (Hetherington, 1983).

Parental attitudes greatly influence the educational aspirations and achievements of adolescents. Girls are usually motivated by the level of education of both parents, whereas boys are more influenced by their father's achievements. The way the parents treat each other and their mutual respect, affection, and concern for each other are highly significant factors in the maturation process of adolescents. Congenial and respectful interparental relationships offer constructive guidance, whereas critical and patronizing sermons are totally counterproductive. The way parents interact with each other and with their children is of crucial importance in the adolescent's attitude toward them, as well as in the adolescent's future behavior in marriage and parenthood (Anthony, 1979; Fleck, 1983).

Quite often adolescents who rebel against parental values and norms come back in adult years to parental values and imitate the parental ways of life. Early adolescents may develop ideas diametrically opposed to those of their parents, thus demonstrating their independence, but ultimately parental moral concepts and behaviors—or lack of them—leave an almost uneraseable impact. Adolescents and young adults are prone to accept the values of the adult society, but they criticize the discrepancy between the professed ideals and actual behavior of adults.

In many primitive societies there are means of normalizing libidinal and aggressive drives. Adolescent girls are usually asked to help assume caretaking responsibilities with the mother, and adolescent boys are expected to help their fathers, allowing them to feel like responsible members of the family (Adler, 1977; Munroe, Munroe, and Whiting, 1981; Warren, 1977).

In contemporary society the formation of the superego in childhood is facilitated by a combination of fear and love for the father, who is perceived by the child as a strong and benevolent figure. Adolescent boys tend to challenge paternal authority, but when the father continues to relate to the son in a friendly and respectful manner, the son may attain a higher level of personality development based not on childish fear and love, but on a more mature friendship and respect for the father (Santrock, 1987; Weiner, 1970).

In most instances a certain degree of indentification with the parents and acceptance of their set of values augurs a better adjustment in the future. Adolescents brought up by parents who "practice what they preach" have a good role model and have a better chance for becoming well-adjusted adults. Even when adolescent boys or girls are somewhat critical of their parents, well-adjusted, open-minded, and sincere parents can still offer useful guidance. Extremely permissive parents offer no guidance to their children, and it is not surprising that their adolescent sons and daughters may rebel against the hollowness of parental lives.

On the other hand, parents who are extreme disciplinarians do not fare better with their children. Some adolescents succumb to parental pressures and never outgrow their childlike dependence, but many an adolescent develops an outright hostile attitude and rebels against the oppressive home environment. Lack of parental affection and understanding, coupled with dictatorial and punitive behavior, makes the adolescent feel rejected and lonely. Many adolescents who grow up in a state of emotional deprivation develop the desire to get even with whoever does not comply with their wishes. Many adolescents who feel rejected by their parents don't have the chance to identify with the cultural and moral values of the adult society and become antisocial sociopaths (Wolman, 1987).

SEPARATION: THE PARENTS

Parents never cease to be parents, but children must grow up and cease to be children. Childhood is a state of dependence; adulthood is a state of self-reliance.

A grown man or a woman who calls their parents every day and needs their guidance and approval has not reached maturity. He or she may be physically and intellectually an adult but emotionally still a child.

The last phase of adolescence and the necessary emotional weaning presents both parents and children with considerable, albeit different, difficulties. Most parents love their children and like to have them nearby. Many parents like to be close to their grown children, ready to help, to guide, and to protect, as they did in the past when their children were young. It is not easy to accept the fact that grown children do not need the help and protection they once did, and they may resent parental guidance. It is quite painful for a parent to realize that a child does not need them any longer and prefers to spend free time with peers and pursuing personal goals.

The realization that one's willingness to help is not welcome may create serious emotional problems for the parents. It may seem unfair that the more you love your children, the more likely you are to get hurt. Some parents dread the feeling of not being needed any longer and resent what they believe to be a lack of gratitude. It is hardly surprising, then, that some parents unwittingly try to perpetuate infantile dependence of their adult sons and daughters. Many of them fail to realize that love must go down the generations. The love parents give to their children must continue and need not be reversed. Children who received plenty of love from their parents will give plenty of love to their spouses and their own children. Children who received little or no love from their parents are likely to become love-hungry "takers," anxious to receive love but unable to give it. Some of them become depressed; some become sociopaths (Wolman, 1973a, 1984b).

SEPARATION: THE SONS AND THE DAUGHTERS

The main difficulty in the separation process is how to break *away* from one's parents without breaking *off* with them. The transition from adolescence to young adulthood involves a critical evaluation of the parents and, at the same time, the start of a mature and friendly interaction with them. The idealized and exaggerated image of the parents in childhood is usually discarded in adolescence and replaced with a hypercritical and rebellious attitude toward "the older generation," which includes the parents.

The transition from adolescence to adulthood, then, is usually associated with a realistic reappraisal and correction of both the idealized childhood identification with—and adolescent rejection of—the parents. Young adults neither idolize nor resent their parents, but by being aware of parental virtues and shortcomings, and remembering what their parents did for them, most young adults are capable of developing a realistic and friendly relationship with them.

The process of weaning and separation is often more difficult for the parents than for the child. The separation process in late adolescence is associated with the overcoming of compliance and conformity on one side and the alienation and re-

jection of parents on the other. Quite often young adults re-embrace parental religions and the moral and cultural values they rejected in adolescence. When parents
are willing and capable of accepting the changing relationship, the separation process is not a separation but the beginning of a friendly interaction between mature
older and mature younger adults (Fleck, 1983; Montemayer, 1983; Steinberg, 1981).

PART II

The Problems of Adolescence

CHAPTER 10

The Body Image

The discrepancy between the speed of biological development and the speed of psychological development is the cause of a great many problems in adolescence. The rapid physical changes in adolescence often cause a great deal of anxiety. Adolescent males and females are concerned with their looks and may feel embarrassed by a sudden increase in the size of the limbs or facial features which seems out of proportion with the rest of the body. Adolescents tend to compare themselves to their peers and worry whenever they notice that they are different from others. Many male adolescents feel that they don't look masculine, that their shoulders are not as broad as those of the other boys, or that their muscles are weak. The speed of development of primary and secondary sexual signs is especially important to them. Some adolescents, males and females alike, tend to withdraw from social life when they believe themselves to be physically abnormal. Their misconceptions about their looks are usually related to speedy or slow physical growth, resulting in larger or smaller noses, chins, ears, limbs, breasts, and penises (Adelson, 1980; Brooks-Gunn and Petersen, 1983; Chumlea, 1982; Lerner and Foch, 1987).

Following the "secular trend" (Roche, 1979), today's American children mature much earlier than they did a generation—and certainly two generations ago (Falkner and Tanner, 1978; Labouvie, 1982). According to Simmons, Blyth, and McKinney (1983), there are significant psychosocial differences between early adolescent boys and girls. Early puberty in boys makes them tend to gain physical strength and puts them in an advantageous position in the peer group, which usually looks up to athletic boys. Early-maturing girls tend to gain weight, which may adversely affect their appearance, placing them at a disadvantage in the peer group. Moreover, girls who menstruate or start to develop breasts at an earlier age are usually unprepared for and often upset by the unexpected biological changes (Ruble and Brooks-Gunn, 1982).

The self-image of early adolescents is often influenced by health problems as well. According to Petersen and Ebata (1988), 11 percent of young adolescents have serious chronic difficulties, 32 percent have more intermittent and probably situational difficulties, and 57 percent have positive, healthy development during early adolescence.

The variety in the speed of biological differences is another factor which affects the adolescent's self-image. Many adolescent boys are perturbed by their small stature, whereas many adolescent girls are upset because they believe themselves to be too tall. It seems that the body image of adolescents is influenced by their belief that all people are supposed to conform to some ideal, average norm (Petersen and Crocket, 1985; Simmons and Blyth, 1988).

APPEARANCE AND SOCIAL RELATIONS

Wishing to look adult and sophisticated, many adolescents tend to imitate adults or try to outdo them. Either type of behavior reflects the desire to conform to the adult society or to surpass it (Hamburg, 1974).

As discussed previously, the development of primary and secondary sex characteristics is influenced by gonadotropic hormones. The parts of the body which are necessary for reproduction, such as the ovaries, uterus, and vagina in females, and the testes and penis in males, as well as the ducts which accompany them, are primary sex characteristics. All other physical changes, such as breasts, pubic hair, facial and axillary hair, and skeletal growth, resulting in widened hips and broader shoulders, are secondary sex characteristics. The wish to impress their peers makes many adolescents view the primary sex characteristics, such as the onset of menstruation in girl, and nocturnal emission in boys, as less important than the appearance of the visible secondary sex characteristics, such as the increase in height and physical strength in both genders, the growth of breasts in girls, and the appearance of facial hair and lowering voice pitch in boys. The way they appear to others is exceedingly important to practically all adolescents (Lerner and Foch, 1987; Ostrov, Offer, and Howard, 1986).

The concern with one's appearance and the impression one makes on others is probably a universal trait, but it is exceedingly important at the time of rapid physical changes, especially when the speed of changes is uneven and does not keep pace with the changes in the appearance of one's peers. In the early stages of adolescence the bodily proportions of the preadolescent become distorted, and most boys and girls are quite unhappy with how they look. A disproportional growth of hands or legs or nose makes them feel inferior to others and causes them to dislike themselves; in some, it may lead to suicidal thoughts (Hamburg, 1974; Lipsitz, 1977; Grumbach, Grave, and Mayer, 1974).

Not all adolescents attach the same importance to their physical appearance.

American boys tend to believe that their physical appearance and prowess will bring them as much success in adult life as it brings them in their peer group in adolescence. American girls tend to expect to win popularity by glamorous make-up, hairstyles, and clothing, and most of them seem to hope that this is what will bring success in adulthood as well. In many instances these beliefs do not originate in the minds of the adolescents, but are products of highly advertised commercials created by adult publications and mass media that stress the importance of impressing other people (Brooks-Gunn and Petersen, 1983).

In other cultures and eras other factors were and are stressed, such as the devotion to the Communist ideology in the former Soviet Union, a hatred of Israel in Arab countries, proper deportment among the higher classes in Victorian England, hunting skills for early American Indians, and the ability to endure pain in ancient Sparta. Apparently, at all ages and in all cultures the adult society sets the standards, and in most situations the adolescent rebellion against traditional values can be stormy but does not last long. Eventually, a vast majority of adolescents do conform with the adult society as they become young adults themselves (Bronfenbrenner, 1970, 1979; Kandel and Lesser, 1972; Mead, 1970; Ostrov, Offer, and Howard, 1986; Warren, 1977).

CHAPTER 11

Emotional Imbalance

INCONSISTENCY

The uneven and irregular process of biological maturation in adolescence is not conducive to balanced and peaceful behavior. The biological rhythm of late childhood is disrupted by spurts of growth, rapid increases in weight, and unpredictable periods of change in metabolism and glandular secretion.

The beginning of adolescence is associated with "organismic disorganization." There is an increase in conflicting emotions, restlessness, impulsiveness, shortened attention span, difficulty in persistent effort, irritability, an increase in masturbation, and often regressive bed-wetting and nail biting (Simmons and Blyth, 1988).

As years pass and the physical and biochemical changes come to an end, the emotional storms also phase out and the adolescent grows into a more balanced adult life. However, the initial steps of adolescence are quite difficult for adolescents and their parents (Jessor and Jessor, 1977; Petersen, 1979, 1988).

Anna Freud (1946) described the transition to adolescence as follows:

Aggressive impulses are intensified to the point of complete unruliness; hunger becomes voracity and the naughtiness of the latency period turns into the criminal behavior of adolescence. . . . Habits of cleanliness, laboriously acquired during the latency period, give place to pleasure in dirt and disorder, and instead of modesty and sympathy we find exhibitionistic tendencies, brutality, and cruelty to animals. (p. 159)

Adolescents may fall in love with someone one day, and dislike the same person the next. Their feelings are volatile and their actions inconsistent, rarely in harmony with their verbal exclamations. Adolescent inconsistency probably reaches its peak in regard to the parents. At one moment the parents are seen in a highly idealized and glorified perspective; at another time they are believed to be tyrannical, unfair, and wretched creatures. Adolescents demand independence from their parents, but at the same time seem to prefer to be dependent on them as well.

The surge of new impulses and the decline in self-control frequently puts the adolescents in frustrating situations. Adolescents tend to harbor exaggerated hopes and to make irrational demands, wanting to carry out plans that are often unreasonable and incompatible with social mores. When their energy is restrained and their whims are not satisfied, adolescents resent the adults who are, or are believed to be, the source of their frustration. Quite often adolescents experience conflicting and seemingly irreconcilable attitudes which may persist until, in later years, they learn to master their inner conflicts and find adult solutions for their problems.

In experimenting with their new independence adolescents need people upon whom they can depend without surrendering their independence. When adolescents meet someone who can accept their need of dependence without questioning their need for independence, they develop a "crush" on that person. When the accepting individual is a person of the same sex, adolescents tend to identify with their idol and imitate the idol's style of dress and mannerisms. If the individual who accepts them is of the opposite sex, the adolescents may show blind devotion to him or her. A "crush" might be a valuable experience for the adolescent, but quite often the recipient may feel embarrassed and reject the adolescent attachment, or in some cases, exploit it in a heterosexual or homosexual way.

AMBIVALENT FEELINGS

Prior to adolescence children's moods and emotions are usually related to real situations and interactions. Preadolescent children feel happy when they are praised by their parents, accepted by their peers, get good marks in school, or have any of their wishes come true, such as getting a coveted dress or having their favorite baseball team win. They feel badly when they are rejected or punished or fail in one of their endeavors. They are angry when frustrated, frightened when threatened, excited or entertained or amused by external events or people. In short, the emotional state of a preadolescent child is usually (but not always) subjective and reflects how adolescents feel about themselves. Adolescents may feel depressed without any objective reason; they may suddenly feel weak, inadequate, and helpless, and shortly thereafter burst with enthusiasm, energy, and self-confidence. They often hate and adore the same things and the same people at the same time. Their involvement with contemporary music in all its present complexity is often an expression of their innermost mood (Blos, 1979; Erikson, 1968; Weiner, 1970).

When boys and girls smoke cigarettes, drink alcohol, and/or take drugs in early adolescence, it is usually out of defiance of the adult society or an attempt to prove to peers that they are "one of the group," "not a kid," and so on. Quite often adolescents use bad language, practice vandalism, skip school, disobey parents and teachers, and use drugs and alcohol in an effort to allay inner anxiety, to overcome feelings of inadequacy and inferiority, and to cope with depression. Adolescents' boisterous behavior and tendency to overreact (to be described later) is often an effort to cover up their feelings of dissatisfaction with themselves.

ANXIETY

One must point out the difference between anxiety and fear. Adolescents are much more prone to anxiety than to fear. Fear is a reaction to danger. When the fear is in response to a real threat and is based on a correct evaluation of one's own resources in comparison to the threat, then the fear is a normal and important adjustive reaction and has survival value. However, when one overestimates the power of threatening people or situations and fears nonexistent dangers, then the fear is irrational and maladjustive.

Anxiety is quite a different emotion. It is a state of diffuse feelings of weakness which are associated with doubting one's ability to cope with any danger and/or to withstand any stressful situation. Anxious individuals underestimate their own resources and feel trapped by whatever adversities they may encounter. Familiarity with a threatening situation and the presence of dependable allies reduces one's fears but does not allay anxiety. Fear comes from without, anxiety comes from within; namely, from one's own unconscious (Wolman, 1978a).

Adolescent moods shift from an unrealistic anxiety to an even more unrealistic, exaggerated self-confidence. Courage implies faith in oneself. It is the feeling that one can "stand up and be counted." Genuine courage is realistic and takes into consideration a fair estimate of one's powers.

Anxiety symptoms are quite frequent in adolescents, and a great many early adolescents experience anxious moods. Depression is less frequent than anxiety, but some periods of "feeling miserable" are typical for boys and especially girls among the 12- to 15-year-old age group. Adolescents are self-conscious, have low self-esteem, and tend to be critical of themselves. Some develop a gloomy outlook on their future, doubt their ability to face adult tasks, and harbor suicidal thoughts (Jacobs, 1971).

Anxiety in adolescents is one of the symptoms of their feelings of inferiority. They wish to be adequate, mature, and self-sufficient adults. However, the adolescent psychological transition from dependence on their parents to adulthood does not lead directly to the mature ideal of accepting one's limitations and inevitable adult *interdependence*. Instead, most often the adolescent rebellion against childlike dependence leads to the wish to be totally *independent*. Naturally, since total independence implies isolation, it is virtually impossible to achieve; this wish never comes true for any of us. Many adolescents feel inadequate and frustrated by their dependence and do not expect much of themselves, since they view their dependence as failure (Bandura, 1982; Seligman and Peterson, 1986).

DEPRESSION

One must draw a distinction between depression and other negative feelings, such as sadness, disappointment, frustration, and so on. Wolman's *Dictionary of Behavioral Science* (1989) defines depression as follows:

> **depression**   Depression, as opposed to other negative feelings such as sadness, unhappiness, frustration, sorrow, or grief, is a feeling of helplessness and blaming oneself for being helpless. Depression is self-directed hatred usually associated with hatred directed toward others. Depression is endogenous when it comes from within; erogenous depression is a reaction to misfortune. Depression is not limited to the classic syndrome of unipolar depressive or bipolar manic-depressive psychosis. People afflicted by a physical disease may feel pain, loneliness, and unhappiness without hating themselves, but if they blame themselves, they are depressed. Depression can be associated with several mental disorders; sociopaths often blame themselves for being weak and try to compensate by overt aggression. Schizophrenics could be more depressed than manic-depressive psychotics, and their depression carries profound feelings of self-hatred.

According to Rutter, Izard, and Read (1986), there are significant gender differences in the frequency and depth of depression. Adolescent girls tend to be depressed more frequently and to a greater degree than adolescent boys. The reason for this difference is related to both genetic and endocrinological factors, as well as to situations of sociopsychological stress. Kandel and Davies (1982), writing about the "epidemiology of depressive mood" in adolescence, found girls to be more susceptible to depression than boys. Also, Petersen and Seligman (1984) maintained that, as a rule, adolescent girls are exposed to a greater challenge than boys; certainly puberty affects girls more than it affects boys and presents a considerable "risk factor for depression." Weissman and Klerman (1977) also stressed sex differences in regard to the epidemiology of depression.

ATTITUDE TOWARD ONESELF

Some authors maintain that overall understanding of self and self-esteem improves as adolescents get older (Damon and Hart, 1982), whereas others report the opposite. For instance, Green and Horton (1982) report that the incidence of mental disorders, drug abuse, and cases of suicide increase as adolescents grow older. Weiner (1980) and Kaplan, Hong, and Weinhold (1984) also report that the frequency of mental disorders among older adolescents is greater than it is among younger adolescents.

THE NEED FOR ATTENTION

Many adolescents tend to believe that others pay as much attention to them and are as preoccupied with their appearance and behavior as are the adolescents themselves. Quite often adolescents act as if they were on a stage, expecting to be admired or criticized by the audience. Adolescents are more concerned with being observed than with observing, and they tend to solicit the opinions of their peers. Many conversations between adolescents are based almost entirely on the question: "What do you think of me?" The opinions expressed are usually quite frank, and not necessarily flattering.

The belief that they are observed by whoever they interact with makes adolescents believe they are indeed "special," or even "unique." When they feel hurt or rejected they are inclined to believe that no one else has ever suffered as much as they have, since their personalities are singular and unprecedented, and thus they assume that no one could possibly understand their problems. Quite often they act in an unrealistic and irresponsible manner in the belief that bad things happen to "other people," but "not to me." When adolescent boys take grave physical risks, such as speeding down a highway, they tend to believe that they are somehow immune to car accidents. Many an adolescent girl who has sexual intercourse without using contraceptives seems to believe that she is "someone special" who is somehow protected, and need not worry about becoming pregnant (Diepold and Young, 1979; Dreyer, 1982; McKenry, Walters, and Johnson, 1979).

Quite often adolescents deny reality and ignore possible consequences of their extensive risk-taking behavior. They seem to need to believe that they are above the rest of average humanity, and often go from the extreme belief in their superiority to an abysmal feeling of inferiority associated with suicidal thoughts and, in some cases, suicidal attempts. The suicidal attempts can be serious, but often they are half-hearted and serve the purpose of warning and/or seeking help from parents and peers. Unfortunately, even melodramatic suicide attempts can be unintentionally fatal (Jacobs, 1971; Wolman and Krauss, 1976).

ALIENATION AND RUNNING AWAY

Some adolescents do not feel socially accepted by their peers. Some of them do not experience the reassuring feeling of belonging to a group and feel rather uncomfortable in the presence of others their own age. Sometimes parental criticism of the adolescent's peers makes the adolescent blame himself or herself for disloyalty to the parents; sometimes the peer group does not offer friendliness and acceptance. The adolescent who feels rejected may reproach himself or herself and perpetuate the isolation, feeling unable to win friends. Quite often, adolescents blame themselves for a true or imaginary lack of social graces. The fear of another rejection or ridicule may prevent the adolescent from seeking affiliation within another group and may help to perpetuate their isolation and loneliness. Some adolescents look over the existing groups and do not find one which could meet their emotional or intellectual needs, and feel alienated and rejected even when no one is actually rejecting them.

Some adolescents harbor conflicting feelings, both craving group affiliation and erecting barriers against becoming members of a group at the same time. Some self-conscious adolescents develop a close relationship with one person of the same or the opposite sex, usually as lonely as they are. Should such a person renege on the relationship, the feeling of rejection can be quite severe.

Some adolescents run away from their parents and some run away from their peers. In the United States every year close to one million adolescents are reported missing and about two hundred thousand are arrested as runaways.

Not all runaways display antisocial attitudes or are involved in illegal behaviors. Though some seem to be running toward alcohol, drugs, and unrestrained sexual freedom and intimacy, many are seeking independence from overprotective parents by searching out new experiences and adventure. Some of them run away from a rejecting home environment, rejecting classroom peers, interparental dissent, broken homes, and other unpleasant situations.

CHAPTER 12

Sexual Problems

THE CHANGING ATTITUDES

Adolescent sexual behavior represents a contradiction of terms in contemporary society. Adolescence is usually defined as a transition from the social status of childhood, which connotes dependence, irresponsibility, and playfulness, to the social status of adulthood, which connotes responsibility and seriousness.

Today we are witnessing a *remarkable process of social change* that involves a wide range of medical, political, economic, educational, sociological, and psychological factors. The social norms that required marriage before the start of sexual behavior are no longer generally accepted, and today's adolescents engage in every type of sexual behavior. Whereas some time ago sexual behavior among adolescents was believed to be deviant, today it is a common occurrence (Chilman, 1983; Dreyer, 1982; Wolman and Money, 1980).

One cannot say that present-day adolescents in general are particularly prone to excessive and uninhibited sexual behavior. No study of the nervous system and biochemistry of the adolescent organism has produced an indication of hypersexuality in adolescence. Sexually provocative styles in fashion are not necessarily a sign of excessive sexuality, nor is provocative dress limited to teenagers (Wolman, 1973b).

Experimental studies have shown that extreme hypersexuality results from the destruction of temporal lobes in cats and rats. Destruction of the area of amygdala in the hypothalamus results in exceedingly receptive sexual behavior in female rats, implying the possibility that the hypothalamus exercises an inhibitory influence on sexual behavior. However, the hypothalamus and the temporal lobes of adolescents function practically the same way as they function in adulthood, and there is no reason to assume mass pathology in all adolescents and a spontaneous cure in adult years (Wolman and Money, 1980).

Apparently, the contemporary changes in sexual behavior in adolescence are a combination of biological and psychosocial factors. The "secular trend" (Roche, 1979), which is the fact that contemporary adolescents reach sexual maturity earlier than previous generations, stimulates early onset of sexual behavior (Chilman, 1983; Chumlea, 1982; Diepold and Young, 1979; Grumbach, Grave, and Mayer, 1974; Hass, 1979; Money, 1980). The sociocultural factor that affects early sexual behavior is related to an atmosphere of disinhibition inherent in the cultural climate of our time. It is a well-known fact that middle-aged men are the main subscribers of the growing number of pornographic publications. Middle-aged men form the core of the immature audiences that fill theaters where pornographic pictures are shown for "mature adults" only (Wolman, 1983).

In America dating begins as early as 10–11 years of age, and by the middle teens there is a great deal of sexual manipulation and intercourse. Kinsey's data gathered in the 1950s concerning the frequency of sexual intercourse in adolescence is dated in the 1990s, where sexual relations among teenagers has become the rule rather than the exception.

MALE–FEMALE DIFFERENCES

For millennia men were believed to be more active, dynamic, dominant, courageous, and aggressive than women, who were believed to be passive, dependent, subservient, emotional, and cowardly. Men were also believed to be more intelligent, more responsible, and more mature than women (Deutsch, 1945; Money, 1980; Wolman and Money, 1980).

All the beliefs in gender differences fall flat in the face of the evidence. There are no gender-specific mental tests, and there is no difference between the IQs of average males and average females. There is no evidence that men are better physicians, psychologists, dentists, lawyers, public leaders, business executives, or experts in any other field or profession than women (Vandenberg and Vogler, 1985).

There are, however, obvious and undeniable male–female differences in regard to sex, procreation, and child care. In coitus the male inserts the penis and the vagina receives it. Intercourse for males usually results in orgasm, but not always for females. Females can have coitus without being sexually aroused; males cannot. Females can "fake" an orgasm; males cannot. Females can have several orgasms, one after another; males rarely have multiple orgasms. Only females menstruate; only females can get pregnant, bear children, and breast-feed them. Males are usually bigger and physically stronger than females, but females live longer than males and have a stronger immune system (Ader, 1981; Shepherd-Look, 1982; Williams, 1979).

Certain aspects of behavior are culturally determined and are a product of learning. For instance, in our culture the stereotyped masculine role is spelled out at an earlier age for boys than for girls, and behavioral demands are made by mothers at a time when a little boy may not be ready to understand what is demanded from him. Sometimes the boy has no pattern to follow. When the father is meek and indecisive, the little boy may become utterly confused in regard to the allegedly aggressive masculinity that is expected from him. It is small wonder that males may have greater difficulty in achieving same-sex identification than females (Unger and Denmark, 1975; Wolman and Money, 1980).

The confusion in parental social roles plays havoc with sex-role identification of the offspring. A domineering, self-righteous mother married to a weak, dependent man often expects her young son to become a "knight in shining armor." It may be that the little boy then identifies with the "strong aggressor" who is his own mother, and the growing number of male homosexuals is a case in point.

Children of both sexes initially identify with the mother because she takes care of them. When the father becomes the chief source of rewards for the male child and participates in many activities with him, the boy gradually identifies with the father. There is a definite relationship between high father-identification and perception of the father as a rewarding and considerate person. The degree of father-identification is highly correlated with masculinity of attitudes.

In order to resolve the Oedipal complex, the adolescent has to ward off both parents. Due to the increased libido, the Oedipal feelings are often intensified in adolescence and must be resolved. Because of an attraction to the parent of the opposite sex which is too great, conscious or unconscious parental gestures which are seductive become quite disturbing to the adolescent.

MASTURBATION

In ancient times masturbation was severely condemned as a sinful waste of sperm in poorly populated areas. Errors die hard, and the idea that masturbation is evil and leads to insanity and/or a host of horrible diseases is still very much alive. Despite all the religious prohibitions, however, masturbation is generally practiced in childhood, adolescence, or any age.

In early adolescence masturbation and sexual experimentation with a friend of the same or opposite sex is a common experience. By the age of 15 about 60 to 80 percent of boys and 40 to 50 percent of girls masturbate. From age 15–19 over 70 percent of boys and over 50 percent of girls masturbate once or more frequently per week. Adolescent males actively engaged in interpersonal sexual relations usually give up masturbation, whereas adolescent females may continue to masturbate, probably to release sexual tension created by sexual activities that do not always bring on an orgasm (Hass, 1979).

Adolescents have mixed feelings about masturbation; should they indulge or control the sexual urge? Most contemporary parents do not threaten their children with visions of insanity, blindness, and other diseases, but usually they express disapproval of masturbation. Hiding masturbatory activities creates additional conflict and increases inner tension and feelings of guilt, which may lead to rather frequent and almost compulsive masturbation.

The opportunity for a frank talk with an understanding adult may relieve the tension and sometimes leads to a decline in masturbation. When masturbation is not frowned at but accepted as a natural temporary relief, it is usually self-terminated with the start of satisfactory interpersonal sexual relations.

Many adolescents try to find reasons for abstaining from masturbation besides the fear of punishment. They rarely succeed and often develop tension, anxiety, and guilt feelings. These guilt feelings do not necessarily continue into adulthood and, as mentioned, with the beginning of adequate interpersonal sexual relations adolescents masturbate infrequently and/or not at all (Dreyer, 1982; Hass, 1979; Shepherd-Look, 1982; Wolman and Money, 1980).

CULTURAL–HISTORICAL COMPARISONS

Sexual behavior is hardly, if ever, culture-free. In ancient times described by the Old Testament, when the earth was badly underpopulated and the very survival of a clan or a tribe depended on the number of working and protecting hands, children were the greatest blessing. Childless women were not respected; the more children a woman bore, the more she was loved by her husband and honored by the society. The greatest blessing given by the Lord to the patriarch Abraham was the promise of having an unlimited number of children.

In those cultures where sexuality is not openly practiced in childhood, sexual instruction is usually given at puberty. For instance, when a Cagaba boy reaches puberty, a priest gives him sexual instruction, and the boy is supposed to have intercourse with a widow; he is then expected to live with her in a specially built hut until he can prove that he is able to have sexual intercourse (Mead, 1949).

Jules and Zunia Henry (1953) observed the play of children of the Pilaga Indians in Argentina. Many of these games were of a sexual nature, and included a good deal of mutual manipulation of genitals. In a game called "the genitalia snatching game," the children tried to grab each other's genitals. Sexual relations in Pilaga start as early as 3 or 4 years of age.

Where children can see the adult sexual act, where sexual conversation and gestures are perfectly open, and the child's life is untrammeled by sexual taboos, it is reasonable to expect that the children should experiment with their sexual apparatus and attempt to imitate adult sexual behavior. This is the case among the Pilaga. Considering the extent of child knowledge about sex and the age at which this knowledge becomes articulate—three years—intercourse in a Pilaga household must not only be visible to the children but carried on with little if any attempt to conceal the act from them. Absolutely no prohibition is placed on the child's sexual activity by the adults, so that the children are at liberty to do what they please. (Henry and Henry, 1953, pp. 298–299)

Among the Lesu aborigines sexual relations are practiced openly, and 4-year-old children imitate the sexual behavior of their parents. In many Melanesian and Polynesian tribes sexual relations among children and teenagers is the general practice. In the Trobriand and Dobu tribes sexual relations are practiced years before puberty, and no special attention is given to the transition from childhood to adulthood (Aries, 1962).

Aries (1962) described the behavior of adolescent boys in Europe in the fifteenth, sixteenth, and seventeenth centuries. The boys drank large quantities of alcoholic beverages, carried weapons to school, had sexual relations with prostitutes, and occasionally raped local girls.

Apparently the patterns of sexual behavior depend greatly on prevailing cultural morals and manners. In Victorian Vienna during Freud's time, sex was taboo, and the adult society frowned on early sexuality and condemned premarital sexual behavior. Adolescents who identified with parental figures and developed a strict superego exercised a good deal of self-restraint. Some of Freud's disciples maintained that sexual intercourse in adolescence may have a "coarsening effect," and some degree of self-restraint was necessary for refinement of erotic life.

DATING

The dating patterns of American adolescents are undergoing substantial changes. The initial age of dating in the 1950s was slightly above 14 years of age for both sexes, and "going steady" was somewhat above 15 years of age. In the 1980s the initial age of dating was about 12 years (Flavell and Markman, 1983; Lerner and Foch, 1987).

American children are expected to be interested in the opposite sex quite early. Their parents and educators organize their social lives in paired groups, and a child who does not pair off with a member of the opposite sex may be excluded from social events and parties. Adult pressure to have children pair off and date starts at the beginning of the teens and increases with the years. Social pressures explain the fact that dating occurs between boys and girls of approximately the same ages (Brooks-Gunn and Petersen, 1983).

Adolescents who begin to date at a relatively early age change their partners often, and thus become acquainted with a number of members of the opposite sex before they go steady. They may go steady at an early age, but in most instances they break up with their partners frequently and return to promiscuity.

Those who begin to date at a relatively late age usually begin to go steady after a short period of dating. Being somewhat more mature, they are more capable of making a lasting choice and tend to marry more quickly than those who began to date at a younger age.

Adolescents of recent foreign origin, as well as those who have large families and/or low socioeconomic status, date later and "go steady" more quickly. Many of them tend to marry without much delay (Chilman, 1978; Dreyer, 1982).

Early dating does not necessarily prove early interest in the opposite sex. Many adolescents, especially females, are more interested in dating and "going steady," as this provides them with a ready date, which is necessary for social events. Moreover, "going steady" gives the adolescent the feeling of being accepted and no longer lonely.

STEADY RELATIONSHIPS

The feeling of being lonely and not understood is a frequent and perplexing occurrence in adolescence. Most adolescents crave a close relationship with someone their age who would share their experiences and understand them. Some adolescents have close friends of the same sex, some of both sexes, some of the opposite sex. Quite often they have only one close relationship that combines sexual intimacy with long conversation aimed at understanding each other's problems, moods, worries, and hopes. The sexual partner is often the most trustworthy person, friend, and confidante. The heterosexual relationships in adolescence are sometimes associated with a strong feeling of inferiority, counteracted by joint participation in a variety of activities and sharing information about oneself. The close relationship offers the opportunity to fulfill the need to express oneself and lends support in the search for identity and the meaning of life.

In many instances, adolescents carry stereotypical ideas of the adult society. Quite often adolescent girls expect their boyfriends to be "more masculine," that is, more outgoing, more self-assertive, less affectionate, less dependent, and less in need of their approval. Many adolescent boys prefer their girlfriends to be "more feminine," that is, passive and affectionate, more subservient, less outgoing, less assertive, less intelligent, and less independent.

SEXUAL INTERCOURSE

The last fifty to sixty years have brought a significant increase in sexual activities in adolescence. The increases for boys are as follows:

- In 1925 about 25 percent of high school boys and 55 percent of male college students had premarital sexual intercourse.
- In 1973 the rates were 55 percent for high school boys and 75 percent for male college students.
- In 1984 the rates were about 60 percent for high school boys and about 80 percent for male college students.

The rates for girls are as follows:

- In 1925 only 10 percent of high school girls and 25 percent of female college students had premarital sexual intercourse.
- In 1973 the rates were 44 percent for high school girls and 70 percent for female college students.
- In 1984, the rates for female adolescents, high school and college age, reached practically the same level as for males.
- At all times the rates for blacks were higher and for whites lower than the national averages. However, over the years the differences are gradually decreasing (Dreyer, 1982; Petersen, 1988).

Apparently, sexual behavior in American adolescents underwent radical changes for both boys and girls, and even more for girls. One can point out several reasons for this change. First, the so-called "secular trend" (Roche, 1979). Contemporary adolescents mature physiologically earlier than their parents and grandparents. Second, the invention of the contraceptive pill, which reduces the fear of pregnancy. The third, and probably the most relevant factor, is the far-reaching change in public opinion. As mentioned, the adult society in the United States has developed a permissive attitude, and although there are quite extreme and confusing differences in public opinion, most parents do not condemn or punish their children for premarital sex.

As far as the adolescents themselves are concerned, most of them tend to approve more of "sex-in-love" with one steady lover than casual and promiscuous relationships. Sexual intercourse is more acceptable when it is a part of a steady, affectionate relationship. Girls are more concerned than boys with having a lasting sexual relationship with someone who cares, but quite a great many adolescent girls practice casual intercourse with several partners.

The first sexual intercourse by male adolescents is usually experienced as supreme pleasure, great achievement, conquest, victory, and proof of their "machismo." Quite often the first sexual intercourse represents to a boy his rebellion against parental controls, an aggressive acting out, and identification with older boys who boast about their true or imaginary sexual prowess and numerous sexual "conquests."

The first sexual intercourse in female adolescents and the loss of virginity often produces feelings of maturity, increased self-esteem, and femininity. There are, however, significant differences in the psychological corollaries of sexual activities between boys and girls. Sometimes a reaction to feeling rejected at home, low self-esteem, or a longing for association with an older boyfriend who provides nurturance, assurance, and affection motivates adolescent girls. Girls who espouse the traditional feminine sexual roles often seek self-realization and feminine identity through a man whom they seek to please and whom they expect to be their future husband. "Liberated" girls are usually more sexually active than the more conservative, "traditional" girls, and for entirely different reasons. Liberated girls pursue their life satisfaction and self-fulfillment in their own efforts rather than through their future husbands. They are therefore less inclined to give in to an affectionate suitor, but they may actively pursue intercourse because it satisfies their own sexual needs. They may also wish to have intercourse when they feel that intercourse is a natural part of a close male-female relationship (Brooks-Gunn and Petersen, 1983; Chilman, 1983; Deaux and Major, 1987; Ember, 1981; Hass, 1979; Petersen, 1979).

THE USE OF CONTRACEPTION

In 1977 the U.S. Supreme Court allowed adolescents to obtain contraceptives without parental consent. However, many adolescent girls seem to believe that they are "low risk" and feel that contraceptives make intercourse less romantic. Presumably, more than 50 percent of unmarried adolescent females do not use contraceptives, and only 20 percent use them consistently. The 15- and 16-year-olds use contraceptives less frequently than the 17- to 19-year-olds. Apparently, the older girls become somewhat more cautious.

It is important to notice that the last fifteen years have brought an increase in the use of contraceptives at all ages. There has been a considerable shift away from the condom, withdrawal, and douching as a means of birth control to the use of birth control pills, diaphragms, and the IUD. The recent epidemics of herpes and AIDS have contributed to an increase in the use of condoms, however.

Some adolescent girls hesitate to use contraceptives for a variety of reasons, such as the cost of the contraceptive, the fear of side effects of the pill and other devices, the fear of future infertility, and the fear of losing the boyfriend who wants sex at a time when she may be unprepared (Zelnik and Kantner, 1980).

ABORTION

In 1973 the U.S. Supreme Court declared unconstitutional all state laws which prohibited abortion during the first three months of a pregnancy. In the last several years the tendency has been for the courts to support the right of pregnant women to decide whether or not to have an abortion. At the present time there are no legal prohibitions against abortion during the first trimester, and in many instances an adolescent can obtain an abortion at a clinic where the fees will be paid by the federal government.

Until the 1973 change in the law, abortion was an illegal, dangerous, and expensive procedure, and abortion rates were highest among middle- and upper-class white women. The abortion rate for teenagers rose by more than 60 percent between 1973 and 1978, and the rate for adolescent females under the age of 15 doubled during the same time. As of 1980, in New York City the rate of abortions per 1,000 live births for women under 19 was 500 for whites, over 800 for Puerto Ricans, and nearly 1,000 for blacks. The national abortion rate is over 30 abortions per 1,000 live births among white women of all ages and over 400 for black women. However, the abortion rates vary from one state to another and from rural to urban areas, are different for the various ethnic groups, and are different from year to year (Dreyer, 1982; Zelnik and Kantner, 1980).

PREGNANCIES

At the present time four out of every ten adolescent girls are likely to become pregnant; most adolescent pregnancies are unplanned and unwanted. In the 1980s there was a considerable rise among white, middle-class girls who believed themselves to be "liberated" and accepted pregnancy and parenthood. The annual rate of adolescent abortion amounts to one-third of all abortions. In the 1980s there were about 1,000,000 annual pregnancies among adolescent girls in the United States, and close to one-half of them ended in abortion. About 250,000 babies were born in the United States out of wedlock, and over 100,000 were born in hurried marriages (McKenry, Walters, and Johnson, 1979).

ADOLESCENT MARRIAGES

About 3 percent of female adolescents aged 14–17 are married. In a vast majority of cases the husbands are much older, and only one half of one percent of boys aged 14–17 are married. Adolescent pregnancy does often lead to marriage, and there is no evidence of abnormality in adolescent girls and boys who marry. In many instances going steady, having sexual relations, and "being in love" with one person is conducive to an early marriage. Early marriages are more frequent among girls who come from families of low socioeconomic status and who have low educational and vocational aspirations (Green and Horton, 1982).

Middle-class adolescents tend to have a more stable and longer-lasting marriage than adolescents of low economic class. The rates of separation and divorce among adolescents are three to four times higher than for people who marry in their twenties. Apparently, the earlier people marry, the more difficult it is for them to cope with the psychological and economic problems of marriage. The rate of divorce is higher when a pregnant girl marries someone whom she would not have married were she not pregnant (Dreyer, 1982).

ADOLESCENTS AS PARENTS

The age of the parents apparently has some impact on the children's physical and mental health. What counts is the emotional relationship between the parents, the parental attitude to their children, the moral and material support of relatives and friends, and a host of psychological, cultural, and economic factors. It seems that 16- or 17-year-old girls can be as affectionate and efficient mothers as mature women, especially when the parents of the young mothers are caring and offer loving help and rational guidance.

Births to teenagers comprise one-fifth of all births in the United States; one-third of all births to adolescent girls are out of wedlock. The majority of adolescent mothers are black, low-income girls. Federal funding for family planning services for single teenagers such as Aid to Families with Dependent Children (AFDC) has alleviated the plight of unmarried mothers somewhat. The rate of illegitimacy has been increasing in the last few decades. In the United States in 1940 the rate of children born out of wedlock to girls 15–19 years old was 7.5 per 1,000 unmarried females; in the 1980s it was almost four times higher. The rate is consistently higher for blacks than for whites. Unmarried adolescent mothers are less likely to finish school than unmarried female adolescents who are not mothers; however, black and white unmarried adolescent mothers do not differ psychologically from their married peers.

A small minority of unwed adolescent mothers give their children up for adoption. The tendency to give the illegitimate child up for adoption is higher among white girls than black girls, who tend to take care of the child. Lately the rate of white girls who raise their babies themselves is definitely growing, and about 85 percent of unmarried black and white adolescent mothers are dedicated, caring, and adequate mothers.

The age of the mother, married or unmarried, might affect the child's physical health, and infant mortality rates for children born to girls under the age of 15 are higher than for the rest of the U.S. population. Children born to girls under the age of 18 have a somewhat higher incidence of learning disabilities, physical illnesses, and handicaps (Dornbusch et al., 1985; Wolman and Stricker, 1983).

CONFUSION OF PSYCHOSEXUAL ROLES: HOMOSEXUALITY

Early adolescent boys engage in homosexual games with some anxiety and guilt, but this does not prevent them from doing so. Horseplay in boys' locker rooms and school lavatories includes exposure and grabbing of genitals and exhibiting erections to one another. Group masturbation, fellatio, and sexual practices may all be tried, and they are not confined to emotionally disturbed boys (Chilman, 1979; Hass, 1979; Wolman and Money, 1980).

Close to 70 percent of 16–19-year-old adolescents do not condemn homosexual relations. Boys seem to be more inclined to accept female homosexuality, whereas girls tend to accept both. Exclusive homosexuality is more frequent among boys than among girls, but the fear of becoming homosexual is more prominent in boys (Wolman and Money, 1980).

In most instances the mothers of homosexual boys are overprotective, domineering, and seductive women who favor their son over their husband. Unwillingly, and most often unwittingly, they encourage feminine activities in their sons and foster a close, affectionate, even confidential relationship with the boy to the exclusion of his father. Maternal overprotection often leads to interference with and discouragement of the boy's contacts with girls. The fathers of homosexual boys are usually weak, passive, uninspiring men who take little or no interest in their sons. It is, however, not entirely proven that the parent–child relationships are the sole cause of homosexuality. Although there is a great deal of evidence that psychosexual identification with the parent of the opposite sex (the Oedipal complex) leads to homosexuality, and most homosexual men have domineering mothers and feeble or absentee fathers, not all men brought up in that sort of environment turn homosexual, nor do all homosexuals have the same family background. Moreover, transient homosexual relations are not necessarily a product of home environment. Many adolescent females engage in occasional sexual contacts with their girlfriends and, as soon as they find a male partner, they develop exclusive heterosexual relations. A similar development takes place in men who engage in transient homosexual relations in adolescence (Drake and McDougall, 1977).

SEXUALLY TRANSMITTED DISEASES

One of the gravest dangers of the rise in premarital sexual intercourse is related to the sharp increase in the incidence of sexually transmitted infectious diseases such as gonorrhea, primary and secondary syphilis, genital herpes and, more recently, acquired immunodeficiency syndrome (AIDS).

CHAPTER 13

Antisocial and
Aggressive Behavior

FROM DEPENDENCE TO DEPENDABILITY

Almost all vertebrates and certainly all mammals are born helpless and need parental care that enables them to reach maturity. Newly-hatched birds and newborn
cubs cannot provide food for themselves; they are too small and too weak, so as
their beaks and teeth and wings and muscles keep growing, they must be taken care
of. When the process of growth and development comes to an end and they reach
the size and strength of other members of their species, they become adults.

Adulthood implies the ability to fight for survival. Animal parents discontinue
their caretaking as soon as the offspring becomes capable of fending for itself.
Higher biological species have a longer way to go from birth to maturity than lower
ones. Human neonates are unable to survive unless they are taken care of, and it
takes a long time before they become adults capable of earning a living and providing a safe place for themselves.

In contemporary societies no one can singlehandedly supply food, clothing, and
housing for oneself. Adulthood today means *interdependence* rather than independence, and the fight for survival is conducted in interaction and cooperation with
other adults.

One has to be physically and mentally mature to be able to provide food, shelter,
and self-defense. During the Industrial Revolution children of poor parents were
forced to work before they were physically and mentally ready to do so, and mortality among these children forced into slave labor reached catastrophic dimensions.

It seems that today we are witnessing a profound discrepancy between biological and sociocultural maturity. Adolescent males and females are not ready or able to assume adult responsibilities, and they remain in a state of dependence despite their apparent biological maturity.

The period of transition from infancy to adulthood becomes prolonged in modern societies. Primitive tribes practiced puberty rites that celebrated a quick transition. The rites were a test of adulthood, and the young man who passed them was admitted to the community of adults. As an adult one is expected to earn his living, to marry, and to support his family. Physical maturity was expected to coincide with sociocultural maturity and, accordingly, the social status is changed from a child to an adult (Adler, 1977; Aries, 1962; Bronfenbrenner, 1970; Kiel, 1964; Munroe, Munroe, and Whiting, 1981; Warren, 1977).

The transition from childhood to adulthood is not an easy task in any society, but the complexity of modern societies has created additional difficulties for youth. The concept of *biological maturation* did not change much in the course of millennia, but the concept of *psychosocial maturity* underwent substantial changes. Contemporary boys and girls in their teens are unable to support themselves, nor are they capable of assuming responsibility for family relationships. A technological society has no use for juvenile shepherds and hunters, and the modern economic system is based on skilled labor and highly qualified managerial and professional cadres. A high school dropout can hardly earn a living in our society, and there are fewer job opportunities for unskilled labor. Prolonged schooling is needed for economic adjustment, and adequate psychocultural maturity is a prerequisite for participation in modern societies. A socioeconomic-cultural maturity requires a high level of psychological development, which cannot be attained in the teenage years.

The *discrepancy between the biopsychological and sociocultural maturity* is aggravated by several factors. One of them is inherent in the "secular trend" (Roche, 1979), that is, in the early biochemical changes at a young age that are accompanied by an abundance of physical and mental energy, aggressiveness, and frequent overestimation of personal potentialities. Adolescent years are a period of frequent conflict, for young people tend to believe that they are adult and should therefore be granted the status of adults.

This process of self-assertion leads to a breaking away from parental authority. Adolescence is the first step of this rebellion and it is usually rather negative; adolescents may try to do whatever seems to be contrary to parental prohibitions and indulge in juvenile pranks, while still depending on their parents economically and psychologically (Adams, 1979; Blos, 1979; Erikson, 1968; Feather, 1980; Grotevant and Cooper, 1983; Lerner and Shea, 1982; Montemayer, 1983; Rutter, 1980).

This "rebellion" against dependence does not make the adolescents independent, but rather enhances their image of *undependability*, irresponsibility, and immaturity. Adult behavior is *dependable*, and young men and women who are gainfully employed and eventually marry and take care of their children are viewed as adults. *They assume adult responsibilities, thus they become mature adults.*

The rebellious attitude in adolescence was described by Schweitzer (1950) in his autobiographical note:

Between my fourteenth and sixteenth years I passed through an unpleasant phase of development, becoming an intolerable nuisance to everybody, especially to my father, through a passion for discussion. On everyone who met me in the street I wanted to inflict thorough-going and closely reasoned considerations on all the questions that were then being generally discussed, in order to expose the errors of the conventional views and get the correct view recognized and appreciated. The joy of seeking for what was true and serviceable had come upon me like a kind of intoxication, and every conversation in which I took part had to go back to fundamentals. . . . I became the disturber of every conversation which was meant to be merely conversation. . . . My aunt scolded me as being insolent, because I wanted to argue out my ideas with grown-up people as though they were of my own age. If we went to pay a visit anywhere, I had to promise my father not to spoil the day for him by "stupid behavior during conversations." (p. 54)

Similar behavioral patterns are typical for many contemporary adolescents in the hippie, punk, and other youth groups. Growing long hair, dressing in a manner adults frown at, using slang language, and acting in a provocative manner are frequent occurrences. Some adolescents go further and turn to antisocial and violent behavior (Binder, 1988).

AGGRESSIVE BEHAVIOR

Aggressive behavior is older than the human race, older than love and sexual behavior, and as old as organic life, for in most instances the intake of food means survival for one organism at the cost of death for the organism that was consumed.

The struggle for food and the fight against being devoured fill most pages in the natural history of the universe. Animals often display aggressive attitudes and kill to eat, but under natural conditions they do not kill members of their own species. Animals may fight against members of their own species for better access to food, water, a place to rest, or sex, but they rarely fight to the death.

Hungry or wounded mammals are prone to fight. Wounded animals will attack a stronger enemy whom they usually fear. An *increased threat to life increases belligerence*, and enraged and desperate animals and men attack friend and foe alike (Goldstein and Segall, 1983).

Animals kill for prey and for defense; they kill true or imaginary foes. The ultimate purpose of killing is not one's own or anyone else's death; death of the enemy is a means toward a goal, and the goal is one's survival or some other need of the individual, such as sex or shelter, or derivatives of these needs, such as control of others, feelings of security, or defense against a common enemy (Bandura, 1973).

WEAKNESS AND HOSTILE FEELINGS

People act upon reality as perceived by them. They may overestimate or underestimate their own power as well as the power of others; they often misconstrue the intentions of others and see friendship where none exists or fear hostility where no hostile action is intended against them (Wolman, 1973c).

No one can be or feel powerful at all times and in all situations, and the estimate of one's power directly affects one's mood. Elation is a product of a high estimate of one's power, depression of one's low self-esteem. In the bipolar disorder the manic mood signals a pathological feeling of omnipotence, and depression indicates morbid self-deprecation.

THE NEED TO ACT OUT

There are two aspects to belligerent behavior in adolescents, namely biopsychological and sociocultural. Adolescents are increasingly aware of the rapidly decreasing difference in the size of the body and physical strength between themselves and their parents. The awareness of large physical size and muscular strength tempts them to rebel against adults who *were* stronger and dominated them, especially parents and teachers. At the same time adolescents are aware of their dependence on parents and teachers, and most adolescents comply with the rules set by these authority figures in their lives.

There are, however, many exceptions. Some high school students overstretch their resources and overdo in rebelling against their parents and teachers. They tend to display exaggerated and irrational self-assertion related to the wish to impress peers by showing off longed-for independence.

The need to act out has several avenues. As a rule, the more powerful one is, the less one needs to show this power. Those who are truly self-assured do not boast about their power. The wealthy do not need to overdress, but a *nouveau riche*, insecure or nervous about their newly-acquired wealth or position, will tend to "show off" expensive garments and jewelry, exaggerating or overemphasizing their prestige. The transition from childhood to adulthood represents a similar transition. The newly-acquired increases in the size of the body and muscular strength lead adolescent males to boast about their physical strength and test it in physical contests and fights; adolescent females may tend to "overdo" make-up and dress, and overemphasize provocative behavior as their bodies go through analogous changes (Wilson and Herrnstein, 1985).

Most male adolescents accept the rules of contest in socially approved sports activities. Some adolescents seek other avenues indicative of their rebellion against the norms of adult society. Antisocial behavior is usually an expression of doing something out of the ordinary, something that will shock their parents and other adults and win the respect and admiration of their peers (Youniss and Smollar, 1985).

THE REBELLION OF YOUTH

There are two more clearly different avenues of "acting out," which lead to violent behavior. Some adolescents believe that their "acting out" is for a lofty ideal, and storm college offices, join radical groups, or take part in terrorist acts. Some adolescents who act out in a disruptive and violent manner, however, are often antisocial sociopaths (Goldstein and Segall, 1983; Wolman, 1987).

There is no doubt that the tendency for violent behavior is universal. The forces of Ares, the symbol of belligerence, are philogenetically older than the forces of Eros, the symbol of love. The ability to hate and fight is far more general than the ability to care and to love. It would be rather naive to hope that the inclination to act violently could be completely eradicated (Bandura, 1973; Petersen and Ebata, 1988; Wolman, 1973c). However, the involvement of adolescents and young adults in radical movements which practice self-righteous and violent behavior requires special attention.

There must be something in our times that encourages males and females from the ages of 16 to 20 to join self-righteous movements that profess idealistic concern for humanity yet practice reckless, antisocial behavior. I have interviewed several college freshmen and sophomores, ages 17–19, who took part in the "rebellion of youth" by storming dean's offices and so on. I spoke to active members of the SDS (Students for Democratic Society) as well. Some of these joined the Weathermen and took part in violent behavior. Most of these young adults were of the upper socioeconomic class, and their parents' income was above average, as was their education.

I am under the impression that their rebellion was against what they perceived as the "nothingness" of their parents' way of life, the moral nihilism of parents who cared only about how to "make a buck" and "how to spend it." Some of these adolescents and young adults spent their childhoods in luxurious dwellings and had their pockets filled with pocket money, but did not mind living in substandard conditions as long as they could pursue pleasures in sex, alcohol, and drugs and make "revolutions" against the "establishment" which was basically comprised of any adult that represented an authority figure to them, or subscribed to the cultural majority. The 16-, 17-, 18-, and 19-year-old hippies, punks, or members of any of the other youth cults believed that they, and only they, were in a position to create a new type of culture. Actually, however, in a vast majority of the cases, the attitudes and actions of the "rebels" were a replica of the hedonistic and egotistic philosophies of their parents (Wolman, 1973b, 1973c, 1982b).

Some college freshmen use phraseology borrowed from Marx and Lenin, talk about socialism and justice, advocate world peace and universal disarmament, and vocally criticize the existing economic and racial injustices. One could believe that the protests and revolutionary zeal reflect intellectual alertness and a genuine desire to improve our social system, that this social criticism and disapproval of injustice might be indicative of possible unselfish tendencies and genuine idealism.

Unfortunately, however, the present-day radical youth movements seem to have no constructive program, and have no blueprint for the future. For better or worse, the revolutionary movements in the past had a plan they tried to implement, a strategy to follow, and a powerful backing among the masses.

TERRORISM

Terrorist groups attract youth for several reasons. First, they offer a purpose, a task to be fulfilled, a goal to be attained. Thus they open an avenue for discharge of abundant energy. Moreover, it is not just the "acting out" typical for early adolescence, but a meaningful form of action that gives the late adolescent a sense of direction and purpose. The political themes and ideals of terrorist organizations (such as, for instance, liberation of the Basques from Spanish domination; the IRA rebelling against the Protestant majority and British rule in Ulster; the destruction of the Jewish state in the midst of the Arab Middle East; the Moslems versus Christians tug-of-war in Lebanon; or the fight of Puerto Rican separatists against the United States) give their participants the feeling of superiority, for they and only they have the courage to fight for an allegedly lofty idea. Acting in a close-knit and disciplined group gives terrorists a feeling of power and security, obliterates guilt feelings for self-righteous violence and murder, and proves to them that one can get away with murder.

There is an almost magnetic attraction to power, but the present-day mushrooming of terrorist groups is related to additional factors, and one of them is the decline of parental guidance and lack of positive values. The fact is that *people whose lives are hollow tend to follow*. Adolescents who have nothing to believe in grasp for straws of phony salvation. Having nothing to strive for they tend to follow cult leaders, pseudo-saints, and dictators who promise a future paradise. Many adolescents seek escape in alcohol and drugs, while others join antisocial cults and terrorist gangs. They join leftist or rightist revolutionary groups in a misguided rebellion against the nothingness of their lives. Many members of the German Baader-Meinhof group were middle- and upper-class young people; the same was true of the Italian Red Brigades; the P.L.O. terrorists were well-fed and rich mercenaries supplied with arms by Libya and by money from Arab governments (Manconi, 1980; Ochberg, 1982; Wolman, 1982b).

Children need moral guidance; adolescents need positive ideals; and all human beings need a revival of the basic principle of civilization that says "thou shalt not"; all must accept the same restrictions that enable people to live together.

In interviewing several members of rebellious and militant youth groups, I have distinguished two different voices in their statements. One was the voice of a genuine desire to find meaning and value in human life in *opposition* to the materialistic hedonism and selfishness of the adult society, and the other was the angry stance of the rebellion against nothingness and lack of moral guidance. But the ideas proposed and methods used boiled down to violent manipulations of the social order and dictatorial aspirations. In a way, they fought for privileges for a small minority that believed in their right to impose their will on the entire society with no respect for democratic social order.

DELINQUENCY

In the United States between 1966 and 1986 the number of arrests of male adolescents almost doubled, and the number of arrests of female adolescents tripled. Blacks constitute over 10 percent of the population in the United States, but black adolescents account for more than 20 percent of arrests. Twenty percent of crime victims are blacks (Binder, 1988).

Some psychologists believe that delinquent behavior is related to low levels of intelligence. Whereas it is true that some less-intelligent individuals tend to associate with delinquent gangs and take part in criminal behavior, a low IQ as such is not conducive to delinquency, nor are all delinquent adolescents less intelligent than all other adolescents (Quay, 1987).

There is no adequate evidence that delinquency is always a direct product of a certain personality makeup (Binder, 1988). However, West and Farrington (1977) summarized their research as follows:

> Without in any way contradicting the importance of social and cultural factors in determining the incidence of delinquency, the results of the present study demonstrate unquestionably but irrefutably, that the individual characteristics of the offender also play a large part. (p. 159)

Moreover, a certain personality type is definitely conducive to delinquency; every sociopath is a potential delinquent. In one of my books I called sociopaths "innocent criminals," for whatever they do they always find a justification. They never feel guilty, and only fear prevents them from violating the law (Wolman, 1973a). In further studies of sociopathic personality (Wolman, 1987) I introduced the "hammer and anvil hypothesis": Whereas one cannot exclude the possibility of a genetic predisposition (the anvil), the child–parent interaction (the hammer) plays the leading role in the etiology of the sociopathic personality. Perez (1978) has advanced adequate proof that delinquent behavior begins at home, when parents fail in their parental role of moral guidance. Several authors have arrived at similar conclusions (Kohlberg, 1976; Quay, 1987; Wolman, 1987).

Adolescent delinquency is often generated by groups or "gangs." There is security in numbers, and a criminal gang offers a better chance for security than a lonely delinquent can muster. Moreover, belonging to a group reduces or even abolishes one's guilt feelings and fear, for if "everybody does it," it cannot be wrong. The leaders of criminal adolescent groups are usually severely maladjusted individuals who introduce alcohol, drugs, and unrestrained and often violent behavior to their followers. Quite often they inspire racial, ethnic, or religious bias and lead their gang to violent confrontations with other gangs (Taifel and Turner, 1986).

Whereas a low socioeconomic environment condones and often fosters overt criminal delinquency, middle- and upper-class environments do not always preclude it. Wealthy adolescents do not practice violent street crime as often, but violate the law by alcoholism, drug use, and reckless driving. Material wealth has never been a guardian of honest behavior (Conger and Miller, 1966).

CHAPTER 14

Alcohol and Drug Abuse

In many instances, adolescents' alcohol abuse conforms with the behavioral patterns of their environment. In the lower socioeconomic classes alcohol abuse tends to start earlier, often in preadolescent years, from the ages of 10 to 12. In the middle and upper classes alcoholism may start two or three years later, depending on parental drinking habits and behavior of the peer group. Suburban, middle-class adolescents are less likely to become alcoholics and their peer groups are less inclined to drink heavily and encourage alcohol use. The urban, lower socioeconomic level peer groups are more conducive to collective abuse of drugs and alcohol, but adolescent alcoholism is not a product of a single cause or totally related to the social environment (Yamaguchi and Kandel, 1984; Zucker and Gomberg, 1986).

Many lower-, middle-, and upper-class parents tend to tolerate and even encourage beer and wine drinking at quite an early age, being unaware of the possibility that this may lead to habit formation and heavy alcohol and drug abuse. At the present time, 40 percent of high school seniors are getting drunk once every two weeks, and 30 percent of them smoke marijuana (Blane and Leonard, 1987; Pattison and Kaufman, 1982).

Quite often alcoholic parents violently object and sternly control adolescent use of marijuana, while they themselves are involved in heavy alcohol abuse. Some adolescents arrive at the conclusion that drinking is the right way for mature people to act. Many adolescents become alcoholics as well, believing that the use of alcohol makes them mature and independent adults (Millman, 1978). About 70 percent of graduating high school seniors use alcohol frequently. Nine out of ten high school seniors have tried alcohol, and six out of ten have used marijuana (Jessor, 1984;

Jessor and Jessor, 1979). Apparently, most adolescents start drinking before reaching 15 years of age.

ETIOLOGIC DETERMINANTS

Presently we are witnessing a growth of attention to the potential role of genetic factors in various aspects of normal and abnormal personality developments (Cattell, 1982; Rose and Ditto, 1983), and several research works have pointed to the possibility of genetic predisposition to alcoholism. Cadoret, Cain, and Grove (1980) studied the development of alcoholism in adoptees whose biological parents were alcoholics. Also, Gurling, Oppenheim, and Murray's (1984) study of twins offered significant support to the theory of the potential role of genetics.

Alcohol abuse is mostly related to environmental influences, and children of alcoholic parents are four times more likely to become alcoholics than the children of non-alcoholic parents. A great many adolescent alcoholics are brought up in an environment where drinking is a general and accepted behavioral pattern.

Mentally disturbed and especially sociopathic adolescents tend to become heavy drinkers, but certainly not all alcoholic adolescents are neurotics and sociopaths (Cloninger and Reich, 1983; Vaillant, 1983). With the exception of genetically determined cases, alcohol addiction in adolescence is not always related to psychopathology, and adolescent alcohol abuse is usually a product of several factors. Adolescent interaction with parents and peers is an important and highly relevant factor in adolescent normal and wayward behavior inclusive of alcohol and drug addiction (Youniss and Smollar, 1985).

DOES ALCOHOLISM LEAD TO PSYCHOPATHOLOGY?

It is hard to keep in mind that both alcohol and drugs can be taken initially for a variety of reasons. Some children and many preadolescents and adolescents experiment with alcohol and drugs to satisfy curiosity, to heighten sensation, to reduce tension, or to improve self-confidence and facilitate social interaction. In many instances preadolescents and adolescents unwillingly and unwittingly develop psychological dependence and become addicted, some to a lesser degree, but some to a serious physical dependence. Not every preadolescent and adolescent who occasionally uses alcohol or drugs will become addicted, however (Schuckitt, 1987).

The intermittent use of alcohol and drugs does not necessarily indicate severe maladjustment and psychopathology. It is still an open question as to what extent alcohol and drug abuse are a product of psychopathologic and especially sociopathic personalities. However, even well-adjusted adolescents who, for a variety of reasons, become alcohol or drug dependent eventually may become maladjusted (Bihari, 1976; Cloninger and Reich, 1983). When they become addicted, their behavioral patterns change, and many substance-dependent adolescents become aggressive, violent, and severely disturbed.

DRUG ADDICTION

Current research on drug addiction in adolescence deals with both biological and sociopsychological factors (Long and Scherl, 1984). The fact that not all adolescents brought up in similar family settings and similar sociocultural environments become drug addicted suggests the possibility of genetic predisposition. Let me repeat here the paradigm of "hammer and anvil." The environmental influences are the hammer, and the blows of the hammer are highly significant etiologic factors. A sturdy anvil can take the blows, whereas a weak anvil will fall apart. In other words, adverse sociopsychological influences cause more damage when the biological background offers limited resilience. Huba and Bender (1982) introduced a multifactor theory of etiology of drug addiction that covers both biological and sociopsychological factors, as drug addiction in adolescence must not be presented as a product of a single factor.

ETIOLOGIC DETERMINANTS

Adults take drugs for a variety of reasons, most of them similar to the reasons that adolescents take drugs. Drugs are taken in order to reduce tension, to overcome anxiety, to boost self-confidence, and to make one feel more active and self-assertive. However, not all people who suffer from insecurity or inferiority feelings and not all depressed individuals seek support in drugs; similarly, not all adolescents, whatever their problems are, turn to drugs.

In most instances drug addiction is a *combination* of biological, psychological, and environmental causes. Many alcohol and drug-addicted adolescents have a history of irresponsible "acting out" and antisocial behavior that could be related to a genetic, biological predisposition that leads them to seek escape in alcohol and drug use. In some cases, however, compulsive substance abuse is related to adverse environmental situations and represents an attempt to escape feelings of rejection and loneliness brought on by low self-esteem and feelings of inferiority (Meyer, 1986; Millman, 1978). In the majority of cases, however, home environment plays a highly significant role in the development of drug addiction in adolescence. Parental drug addiction serves as an invitation to preadolescents and adolescents to follow in their parents' footsteps.

PREVALENT DRUGS

Today drug abuse is a major health crisis which is rapidly spreading across the United States. In addition to the enormous amounts of drugs which are manufactured here illegally, or prescribed and issued for medical reasons and then subsequently misused, there is a black market in illegal drugs which are imported from other countries. The import of these illegal drugs has become one of the major booming financial enterprises for these poorer countries, which makes containment extremely difficult; attempts at halting or curtailing the flow of illegal drug traffic into this country has rapidly escalated to the level of a "war on drugs."

The easy availability and economic opportunism of the drug trade is only one facet of this critical social dilemma, however. The use of drugs has expanded to include all socioeconomic classes and occupations, from assembly-line workers to CEOs. Whether the demand for drugs has caused their accessibility or the abundance of drugs has created the demand is entirely academic at this point. The fact is that more than 57 million Americans over the age of 12 have smoked marijuana, and 22 million have used cocaine. The extensive use of drugs in the 1960s and 1970s has produced a current society of adults who, while they may ostensibly favor strict laws forbidding the use of drugs, are inadvertently providing their adolescent children with substance-abusing role models, and often the substance itself—from their own liquor cabinets, medicine chests, drawers, and "stashes" (Carper, 1987).

Alcohol and marijuana are the first choices for initial experimentation in adolescence, and the use of both increases with age. "Grass" belongs to a family of drugs identified as *Cannabis*, which includes hashish, hashish oil, and tetrahydrocannabinol, or THC, which is the active ingredient in marijuana and hashish. Though a tolerance to the drug can be built up, the degree of physical or psychological dependence is unknown. It causes euphoria, relaxed inhibitions and bursts of laughter, increased appetite, distortions of the perception of time, and disoriented behavior. An overdose can cause fatigue and paranoia and even possible psychosis, while heavy, long-term use can be linked with mental deterioration. Marijuana is exceedingly popular with high school students, and in many places has already reached grammar school children. At the present time 20 percent of adolescents between the ages of 12 and 18 and 40 percent between the ages of 16 and 18 use marijuana. The effects of marijuana depend on the strength, frequency, and quality smoked, and also on the psychological makeup of the individual. Many experience feelings of omnipotence and become cocky and aggressive (some even hallucinate); after awhile they usually become sleepy, and even stuporous. Quite often pushers will sell teenagers contaminated or altered substances, substituting marijuana with a weed or tobacco impregnated with a hallucinogen such as dimethyltryptamine (DMT) (Adelson, 1980).

Depressants make adolescents feel sociable, relaxed, and in a "good mood," but affect their reasoning ability, motor coordination, and speech in much the same way that alcohol does. Barbiturates (or "downers" and "goofballs"), benzodiazepines (such as Valium, Ativan, and Librium), chloral hydrate, and methaqualone (better known as Quaaludes or "ludes") are all part of the depressant family of drugs, and all produce various degrees of both physical and psychological dependence. Prolonged use can cause withdrawal symptoms, and death can occur from either overdosing or mixing with other drugs or alcohol.

Stimulants such as phenmetrazine (Preludin), methylphenidate (Ritalin), and amphetamines (commonly referred to as "speed") are frequently used by adolescents, often as a study aid, or by adolescent females in an attempt to lose weight. Often prescribed for "medical" reasons, these and tranquilizers (depressants) are substances frequently found in parental medicine chests. The use of this drug causes increased alertness and excitation resulting in long periods without sleep, talkativeness, euphoria, an increase in pulse and blood pressure, and an almost total loss of appetite. It produces a feeling of power and control, although users become very tense, restless, and sometimes paranoid. The "crash" when the substance leaves the body can be quite severe, however, leading to feelings of exhaustion and depression. Overdosing can cause convulsions, hallucinations, and possible death. Cocaine is a stimulant, even though it is wrongly designated as a narcotic under federal law. About 4 percent of adolescents under the age of 18 use cocaine, which produces a "high" similar to amphetamines, but more euphoric and of extremely short duration. Cocaine users tend to suffer from severe bouts of depression and can develop tachycardia, as cocaine speeds up the heart rate tremendously; used in conjunction with other substances it can produce serious, sometimes fatal results. The psychological dependence on these drugs is extremely high, and while there is some evidence that there is a physical addiction or buildup of tolerance with cocaine, the degree of physical dependence on this drug and other stimulants is still a matter of controversy.

The LSD "trips" of the 1960s and 1970s paved the way for a new generation of *hallucinogens*, now sometimes referred to as "designer drugs." Hallucinogens include mescaline and peyote, LSD, phencyclidine, PCP, "Angel Dust," and "Ecstasy"; all cause illusions, delusions, hallucinations, and poor perception of time and distance. There is very little data to support a physical or psychological dependence on these drugs. An overdose can cause a more intense "trip," and result in psychosis and possible death. Adolescents rarely use hallucinogens outside of small, controlled groups of friends because the behavior is so radically changed; it is, however, sometimes used as a "party" or "club" drug.

Drug abuse and addiction in adolescence has often been related to "slum areas," lower levels of economic and academic opportunity. Today it is a middle- and upper-class problem as well; even a drug such as heroin, though still primarily identified as a heavy "street drug," is now being used by successful middle-class professionals and their children. Heroin is a *narcotic*, one of a group of drugs that includes opium, morphine, codeine, methadone, and hydromorphine (Dilaudid), which are both physically and psychologically addictive. Their general effect is one of euphoria, languor or drowsiness, respiratory depression, constricted pupils, and lack of appetite. Heroin overdose is one of the main causes of death of adolescents in New York City. Many adolescents from the ages of 12 to 18 take heroin; the national rate is over 1 percent for heroin and about 6 percent for other narcotics. Every year agents of the U.S. government seize thousands of tons of heroin smuggled from abroad, and thousands of adolescents become addicted.

Even these alarming figures do not accurately reflect the gravity of the situation, however, as drug abuse is rarely restricted to just *one* drug. The average adolescent who enters a substance abuse treatment program is on five different drugs and is a heavy user of alcohol as well. Children brought up in a permissive and commit-ment-free atmosphere start experimenting at the age of 10 to 13 with alcohol and "grass," which may lead to more powerful drugs such as amphetamines, cocaine, crack, crank, heroin, LSD, and other "designer drugs." Lack of self-control and the inability to cope with their problems is a relevant factor in adolescent drug abuse, but its origins are in the adult society and the general decline of self-discipline (Baker and Cannon, 1987; Bihari, 1976; Carper, 1987; Long and Scherl, 1984; Meyer, 1986; Millman, 1978; Shiffman and Willis, 1985; Yamaguchi and Kandel, 1984).

PART III

Causes and Remedies

CHAPTER 15

The Changing Organism

GENETIC PREDISPOSITION

The main cause of adolescent problems is the biological transition from childhood to adulthood. The rapid and rather uneven changes in the size of the body and in its inner organs, the maturation of the sexual reproductive system, and the overall increase of physical and mental energy greatly contribute to an adolescent's difficulties. One may compare these changes to a substantial increase in the power of a car engine without a proportionate increase in the power of brakes and steering wheel (Carron and Bailey, 1974; Chumlea, 1982; Coleman, 1974).

Freud's tripartite personality model includes the impulsive *id*, which needs instant gratification, the reality-oriented *ego*, which forces postponement and modification of the id wishes, and the *superego*, which is a self-control system derived from identification with one's parents (Freud, 1938). Adolescence seems to be a partial regression to the infantile id-behavior with inadequate ego controls and shrinking superego controls. The increased physical strength and the powerful drives challenge the immature and not yet adult ego, and the rebellion against parental domination plays havoc with the restraining role of the superego. The identification with the peer group and the emerging "we-ego" adds to adolescents' feeling of power and often incites them to irresponsible risk-taking and brazen actions (Blos, 1979; Freud, 1958).

The gulf between the ages of physiological and psychological maturation creates additional problems. One hundred years ago the age of menarche in the United States and Europe was about 15–17; today it is 12–14 years of age. A similar "secular trend" applies to boys. The tendency to an early start of sexual relations creates a great many problems (Eveleth and Tanner, 1976; Hass, 1979; Roche, 1979).

In some instances disturbed behavior in adolescence is caused by organic factors. Just at the onset or closely before the onset of puberty some children whose testosterone and estrogen secretions are previously elevated display impulsive and volatile behavior and may become quite aggressive (Grumbach, Grave, and Mayer, 1974; Lerner and Foch, 1987; Winter, 1978; Wolman, 1973a, 1973b).

Organic brain syndrome, minimal brain dysfunction, or other neurological abnormalities may cause a variety of disturbed behaviors, such as hyperactivity, excitability, poor motor coordination, slow learning, and inadequate self-control. Hyperactivity, impulsiveness, and aggressiveness are stimulated by excitatory neurotransmitters and controlled by inhibitory discharges such as Gaba (gamma-aminobutyric acid). An imbalance of the excitatory and inhibitory discharges may lead to *seizure disorders*. Close to 30 percent of highly violent adolescents have a grossly abnormal EEG, and some have a history of psychomotor epilepsy (Matarazzo et al., 1984).

Violent and delinquent behavior, especially when it is extreme and continuous, is often a product of genetic factors. The criminal records of dizygous (non-identical) twins is 12.5 percent, whereas the criminal records of monozygous (identical) twins is 36 percent, almost three times as high. Apparently, genetics has a lot to do with adolescent behavior. A study conducted in Denmark of adopted boys revealed that the criminal records of boys whose biological fathers had no criminal record was 10 percent, irrespective of the records of the men who adopted them. However, 20 percent of the boys whose biological fathers had criminal records and 35 percent of the boys whose biological and adoptive fathers both had criminal records were delinquent (Binder, 1988; Fuller and Simmell, 1983; Quay, 1987; Wolman, 1987).

Usually there is a good deal of interaction between genetic disposition and environmental influences. Children whose impulsive and disruptive behavior is met with impulsive and punitive behavior by their parents become more belligerent and more difficult to handle. Physical punishment teaches the child that "might makes right," and when the child reaches the teens he or she may repeat the patterns of physical violence.

Close to 80 percent of violent adolescents have experienced violence directed toward themselves by their parents or others, or have witnessed extreme interparental violence or violence in their close environment (Quay, 1987).

CHAPTER 16

Psychosocial Issues

CULTURAL DIFFERENCES

Some authors maintain that the phenomenon of adolescence is universal and only moderately affected by cultural determinants. Kiell (1964) amassed a number of autobiographies, diaries, and letters from diverse societies, from the first century of the Christian era until the present time, to prove that adolescents have always acted in quite the same way.

Studies of primitive societies demonstrate that the transition from childhood to adulthood has always created some problems, but in some primitive societies there was no gulf between biological and psychosocial maturation; thus the problems were quite mild and perhaps did not exist at all (Aries, 1962; Ember, 1981; Henry and Henry, 1953; Munroe, Munroe, and Whiting, 1981; Segall, 1986).

The ideas and behavioral patterns of adolescents originate in the adult society; adolescents tend to absorb the cultural values given to them by adults (Anthony, 1979). Each culture develops its own conceptual systems; thus California Indian tribes viewed menstruation as dangerous because of its alleged impact of anti-fertility; among the Apache Indians menstruation was considered to be a supernatural blessing; and in the Gilbert Islands menstruating girls were considered to be especially susceptible to enemy magic (Mead, 1949; Munroe, Munroe, and Whiting, 1981).

In contrast to the clear demands of primitive societies, adolescents in the United States are confronted with confusing choice situations in a society full of conflicting and often incongruous values. An early imitation of adult behavior, including smoking, drinking, dating, sexual relations, and so on, together with an increased expectation for prolonged education, have created what seems to be a never-ending period of adolescence (Mead, 1970).

CULTURAL DIFFERENCES

Modern adolescents do not create social order, nor do they establish cultural and moral norms. They are born into an existing sociocultural system. They learn manners and morals from their parents, teachers, mass media, and society at large. Sometimes they accept what is given to them, sometimes they modify it, and sometimes they raise their voices in protest. A complete rejection of the past has never occurred; even the boldest revolutions have only removed or added a few bricks to the existing sociocultural structure. Revolutions are full of promises, but the promised "paradise" has never truly come to pass. Consider, for example, the great French Revolution. Despite the high-sounding slogans "Liberte, Egalite, Fraternite," there was precious little freedom or equality granted, and not one iota of brotherhood. There was, however, an indisputable continuity of the French language, literature, and cultural tradition that no revolutionary movement would or could eradicate.

Consider the Soviet Revolution as well. The autocratic Czarist system was abolished and the landowners expropriated. Russia was no longer ruled by a dynasty of tyrants backed by the Byzantine religious doctrine of supremacy of the ruler. Instead it was ruled by a group of party leaders backed by a Marxist-Leninist doctrine of dictatorship. Though the Byzantine tradition of religious supremacy of the ruler was radically changed in the former Soviet Union, the modern party leaders still attempted to exercise a charismatic power.

It is an undeniable fact that sociopolitical changes have a considerable impact on adolescents' way of thinking, their loyalties or disloyalties, and their adjustment or maladjustment (Bronfenbrenner, 1970; Feather, 1980; Kandel and Lesser, 1972; Ostrov, Offer, and Howard, 1986; Rutter, 1980). It is still an open question as to how far the changes go, whether the revolutions are as "revolutionary" as they are believed to be. Contemporary revolutionary youth might be caught up in the social climate of the materialistic group mentality of the adult society. The following quotes from Lynd's *Knowledge for What* (1946) illustrate the point of contemporary society's life of the "double standard":

> The family is our basic institution and the sacred core of our national life. But: *Business is our most important institution . . . other institutions must conform to its needs.*

> Life would not be tolerable if we did not believe in progress and know that things are getting better. But: *The old, tried fundamentals are best; and it is a mistake for busybodies to try to change things too fast or to upset the fundamentals.*

Honesty is the best policy. But: *Business is business, and a businessman would be a fool if he didn't cover his hand.*

Science is a fine thing in its place and our future depends on it. But: *Science has not the right to interfere with such things as business and our other fundamental institutions.*

Patriotism and public service are fine things. But: *Of course, a man has to look out for himself.*

The American judicial system insures justice to every man, rich or poor. But: *A man is a fool not to hire the best lawyer he can afford.*

MASS MEDIA

Social psychologists and sociologists who stress the role of mass media in shaping socially accepted norms often overlook the fact that the deluge of violence and pornography is man-made and could be restrained. The fact is, if no one watched or listened to the disturbing or nonsensical programming now available through television and the radio, it would soon disappear. If children spend hours glued to their seats watching television, it is either because their parents do the same or because their parents wish their children to watch television in order to escape the necessity of interacting or dealing with them. Whatever the content of television and radio, it is the adult society that produces these programs, and the adult society that accepts and promotes them. Adult decisions activate the flood of communication, and it is up to the adult society to monitor, improve, and/or change the content transmitted by this powerful media.

Mass media usually cater to the "lowest common denominator" because they are completely oriented to profit. Programming is geared toward a lower socioeconomic group with less education because this represents the largest portion of society, and therefore more profit for the advertisers who support the program. Thus, this powerful influence often infantilizes its entire audience, for mature individuals are not interested in heightened violent crime and overplayed sexuality. However, children and adolescents who are exposed to television perceive these messages as carriers of the accepted values of the society the adolescents wish to join (Wolman, 1987).

PUBLIC APATHY AND ACCEPTANCE OF CRIME

Today every single citizen of the United States may expect to become the victim of a serious crime at least once in his or her life. According to the Federal Bureau of Investigation, someone in the United States will be murdered every 60 minutes, raped every 40 minutes, robbed every 6 minutes, and burglarized every 40 seconds. Every minute a car is stolen, and every fourth minute someone undergoes a beating that can later be described as "aggravated assault." The surge in violent crime has, in fact, assumed epidemic proportions, and the public seems to have accepted crime as a matter of daily routine (Bandura, 1973; Goldstein and Segall, 1983).

In an article called "Study of the Sickness Called Apathy," A.M. Rosenthal (1964) described the murder of a 28-year-old woman:

> On the night of March 13, 1964, about 3:00 A.M. Catherine Genovese was returning to her home. She worked late as a manager of a bar in Hollis, another part of Queens. She parked her car and started to walk to her death. Lurking near the parking lot was a man. Miss Genovese saw him in the shadows and walked toward a police box. He pursued her and stabbed her. She screamed, "Oh my God, he stabbed me! Please help me! Please help me!" Somebody threw open a window and a man called out: "Let that girl alone!!!" Other lights turned on, other windows were raised. The attacker got into a car and drove away. A bus passed. The attacker drove back, got out, searched out Miss Genovese in the back of an apartment building where she had crawled for safety, stabbed her again, drove away again. The first attack came at 3:15 A.M. The first call to the police came at 3:50 A.M. Police arrived within two minutes, they say. Miss Genovese was dead.

Thirty-eight people heard her calls for help or saw her stabbed on the street near her home in Kew Gardens, but no one defended her nor did anyone call the police.

A patrolman, Norman Brown, told the court that he had come on duty on May 4, 1964, at 4:00 P.M., when he saw a throng of people outside 559 East Tremont Avenue in the Bronx and heard screams. He pushed away the onlookers and found a naked girl on the floor inside. According to Brown, "There must have been 20 people outside and 20 looking down from the second floor landing, but not even one tried to save her from the rapist."

Adams (1964) questioned 40 people who passively witnessed this crime and did not even attempt to call the police. The answers he received were similar to the ones given by the witnesses to the Kitty Genovese murder:

> You look out for yourself today. It was bad for business. How can I make a dollar when I am in court as a witness?

> I'm a man. If I do anything, I get accused of being on the scene.

> Would I have helped her? Mister, if she was screaming rape right now out there, I wouldn't help her. You know why? Because along comes a cop and sees you trying to help and, bang, you get accused for being there.

Again, citing adolescent apathy and antisocial behavior as part and parcel of the many problems inherent in today's modern society conceals the larger part of the truth. Adolescents are a reflection of the adult society; their apathy and lack of morality as evidenced by the rising statistics of delinquency and teenage crime mirrors parental values and actions (Ajzen and Fishbein, 1977; Beech and Schoeppe, 1974; Hogan and Emier, 1978; Kohlberg, 1976; Wilson and Herrnstein, 1985; Wolman, 1987).

SOCIOECONOMIC FACTORS

Over two-thirds of adolescents live in metropolitan areas. One out of six adolescents changes his or her residence every year. About 50 percent of black adolescents live with both parents, compared to over 80 percent of white adolescents (Dornbusch et al., 1985).

There is no evidence that low levels of income and poverty are the main cause of antisocial behavior. Many countries with a low per capita income have a much lower rate of crime than the United States. Moreover, the rate of crime in the 1930s, during the Great Depression, was lower than it is today.

At the present time the widening gulf between income levels and standards of living may create hostile feelings that contribute to antisocial behavior. Lack of opportunities, feelings of helplessness and depression, and exposure to antisocial adults are conducive to delinquency. About 15 percent of adolescents in the United States are living below the poverty level. The ratio of poverty for black adolescents is two and one-half times higher than for white adolescents (Jessor and Jessor, 1979; Kessler and McLeod, 1985; Rainwater, 1970).

Most adolescents are status-conscious. Quite often they try to compensate and overcompensate when they believe their social status is inferior, especially in terms of occupation and income level of their parents and themselves. Fifteen percent of the American population live in substandard conditions, and many of them, especially minorities, live in outright poverty. Many adolescents grow up in slum areas and have little hope or opportunity for success, which causes them to view the middle and upper classes with envy and hostility. Many of these underprivileged adolescents feel alienated and resent the slum areas they live in, their unemployment and poverty. They crave a radical change in their living conditions, and thus some of them practice antisocial and violent behavior (Binder, 1988; Kaplan, 1980; Perez, 1978; Rainwater, 1970; Wilson and Herrnstein, 1985).

ALIENATION

The term "alienation" is often used in a loose and perhaps ambiguous way. If the term "alienation" is used to describe estrangement, breaking away, and becoming different, contemporary adolescents are anything but alienated. Many of them, especially in poverty-stricken areas, live in a mental vacuum created by their parents and drift aimlessly into the same patterns of sexual abuse, senseless violence, and drug addiction they see around them. They are not alienated, however; they are following accepted patterns that are somehow tolerated by large segments of the population.

Alienation means a loss of the feeling of belonging, but many adolescents have never had a chance to *develop* a feeling of belonging. People develop attachments to their family, to their neighbors, to their place of birth, nation, and faith. People who feel that they belong are usually willing to give, to sacrifice, and to be of service. Many American adolescents, and not only minority groups, are not receiving the parental guidance which leads to prosocial behavior; a shifting and/or unstable family structure due to divorce or remarriage, the high incidence of geographical relocation, and a decline in cultural or religious faith leaves nothing to be alienated from (Adams, 1979; Bengtson and Troll, 1978; Conger and Miller, 1966; Grotevant and Cooper, 1983; Van Hasselt and Hersen, 1987; Wolman, 1973b).

FAILURE OF IDENTIFICATION

The quest for identity is often frustrated in a society where parents and society at large do not offer guidance to the younger generation. The natural developmental process and properly guided learning experiences could enable adolescents to embrace idealistic and caring attitudes. Infancy is mainly *instrumental*, with an emphasis on the satisfaction of the infant's needs; in adolescence the give-and-take *mutual* relationship comes to the fore in friendship bonds and groups. In the late phase of adolescence *vectorial* tendencies appear, and many adolescents desire to be of help to humanity if proper guidance is offered to them. Given the proper opportunities and guidance, they would champion the causes of justice and progress, and admire and emulate honesty, friendliness, and courage as virtues related to maturity (Wolman, 1982a).

When they fail to find support for these positive values, when their parents and other adults preach but do not practice moral ideals, many adolescents regress to earlier, immature behavioral patterns. In many instances their parents are unable to serve as adequate role models. Their adolescent children, boys and girls, may have great difficulty in developing realistic attitudes toward themselves and society at large, and some of them become rebellious and antisocial (Bandura and Walters, 1963; Conger and Miller, 1966; Goldstein and Segall, 1983; Klineberg et al., 1979; Rutter, 1980; Wolman, 1982b).

THE CHANGING FAMILY LIFE

Ideally, marriage is a relationship based on reciprocal love and respect for each other's rights. To love means to care and to do the utmost to make the life of one's partner as enjoyable as possible. In a mature marriage both partners are willing to do whatever they can for the other, expecting the same in return. Such an interdependent relationship enables a married couple to welcome, properly care for, and love their child.

No family can be perfect, but contemporary families are facing serious and hitherto unknown problems. The European and American families in the not-too-distant past were large sociocultural units, usually occupying a group of farmhouses or a city block. People tended to marry their neighbors or acquaintances, and the new family ties were added to the old ones. Family connections led to the formation of a clan with grandparents, parents, uncles, aunts, in-laws, cousins, and scores of relatives. The father worked near the home and came home for lunch and dinner; the mother was always home. The children spent most of their time with their parents, relatives, and neighbors, and learned the chores, responsibilities, and joys of adult life by direct observation and frequent participation. Psychosexual roles were closely defined; the boys did not have to learn "masculinity" by watching football and "cops and robbers," but by helping their father in a workshop or on the farm or by joining him in his work around the house. Father's trade or business was usually continued by his sons, who were able to resolve their Oedipal problems through fear of and admiration for the beloved and indisputable head of the family. The boys also had several other alternatives in accepting a masculine role, since there were a number of different male role models to choose from in the family unit in the form of uncles, in-laws, grandparents, and older siblings.

Girls learned feminine manners not by watching glamorous fashion models on television, but by helping their mothers mind the house and take care of the younger children. They too had a choice of role models to identify with in addition to the mother: aunts, sisters, sisters-in-law, cousins, and again, the grandparents.

Jewish, Italian, and Irish immigrants of a generation ago carried the tradition of a "clan-type" family on in the American scene and perpetuated it for awhile, but the current trend is leading toward the small, often isolated "nuclear" family unit (Wolman and Stricker, 1983), where interdependence and identification with a number of extended family members is not possible, and a sense of cultural and familial stability and permanence is all but lost or considerably reduced (Petersen and Spiga, 1982).

THE TECHNOLOGICAL REVOLUTION

The industrial-technological revolution has wrought havoc with the traditional family structure. Fathers do not work near their living quarters any longer, and many of them travel an hour or two each way to their jobs. They leave their homes early in the morning and return late in the evening. Many of them are too tired to talk and play with their children and are happy to put the entire responsibility on their wives' shoulders. On weekends the fathers may feel obliged to go with their sons to a ball game or occasionally take the entire family out for a weekend picnic. Some fathers feel that they deserve weekend entertainment and rest, and leave their homes on weekends for fishing, golfing, or drinking with friends. Less ambitious men sleep on weekends, deepening the gulf between themselves and the rest of their family (Carter and Goldrich, 1980).

Modern women are exposed to more hardships than their mothers were, and face more difficulties than contemporary men. Though technological progress has brought with it electric and gas stoves, dishwashers, vacuum cleaners, and washing machines, it has forced women to join men in the struggle for daily bread. Most women in low economic brackets and many women in middle economic brackets work outside their homes and participate in supporting the family. In low-income families the children are often left alone; middle- and upper-class women hire nurses and household help (Crosby 1982).

Today practically all women rebel against their past subservient role, and the so-called "male supremacy" is facing a hitherto unknown challenge (De Beauvoir, 1953; Unger and Denmark, 1975; Wolman, 1978b).

THE NUCLEAR FAMILY

The technological revolution disrupted the large "clan-type" family. A factory with thousands of employees cannot provide quarters for them around its main buildings the way the old-time farms or ranches provided nearby living quarters for their workers. The distances between the household and the place of work have extended to a number of miles and commuting hours, and skilled technicians, engineers, and executives may not find proper jobs anywhere near their home. The concentration of trade and business in selected areas pushes the residential areas farther and farther away, and very few people can live next door to their place of work today.

Brothers, sisters, uncles, and aunts have had to migrate to distant places and keep contact by mail, telephone calls, and rare "family reunions." The present-day "nuclear family" is comprised of a father, a mother, and their children, now usually two, as opposed to three or four in the 1950s, and a greater number in the eras preceding the twentieth century. Confined to close and exclusive proximity, the members of a nuclear family have no other outlet or resource but each other; there is no "extended family" to help assume caretaking responsibilities or provide interaction, advice, and support. Faced with this kind of isolation, it is small wonder that members of such a small family unit might feel overwhelmed and unable to cope. In such an atmosphere minor misunderstandings easily turn into major conflicts, which may often lead one or more of the family to a doctor's office for private or family psychotherapy (Goldstein, 1988; Jacob, 1975; Wolman and Stricker, 1983).

CONFUSION IN SOCIAL ROLES

The traditional roles of men and women have undergone profound changes in our times. Technological developments and automation have reduced the need for physical strength in industry and increased the need for advanced intellectual ability. Men are generally physically stronger than women, but there are no differences in IQ between them (Wolman, 1985). The growing need for white-collar and public service workers has opened doors to gainful employment for millions of women, and the need for a second income to support the family has caused millions of women to seek gainful employment.

The idea of "male supremacy" is a myth of bygone days, and contemporary women compete with men in all fields of trade, the professions, the sciences, the arts, and in all aspects of economic, cultural, and political life. These changes are gradually being accepted by male society, though women's interest groups must still fight vigorously for equal opportunities and equal pay (Unger and Denmark, 1975).

In the area of family life this change in attitudes meets with more resistance. Many men still, consciously or unconsciously, want to be looked up to and admired as if they were still the leader of the family. At the same time, their reduced economic power and time spent with their families is, ironically, leading to a substantial decline in their prestige within the family unit. This growing dissonance in marital relations often leads to divorce, and significantly contributes to the problems of adolescents. In my office I have often heard severe accusations against prominent businessmen voiced by members of their disgruntled families and, vice versa, disenchanted executives and professionals complaining about a lack of respect and affection on the part of their wives and children.

Apparently, business and professional competence and success have little, if any, impact on interfamilial relationships. The wives of unsuccessful men are unhappy with their economic position, and the wives of highly successful men often complain about the lack of interest, coldness, and aloofness of their husbands. The difficulties are aggravated by the inadequate attention many men give to their wives and children, and the double role women are now undertaking. In many instances, the modern mother is expected to be a tough breadwinner who competes with men, a sweet and soothing wife, and the controlling, nurturing, and decision-making parent. Torn between their conflicting roles as breadwinners and professionals on one side, and their mother-wife status on the other, many modern women find it difficult to cope with these dual obligations (Crosby, 1982).

The situation becomes quite serious when either the husband, the wife, or both carry the seeds of immaturity left from their own childhood. Born in parental dissent, brought up in a home with declining parental authority and confused maternal role, many men and women expect in marriage what no marriage can offer. Disappointed in their own parents, many of them hope to find in their spouses what they have missed in childhood, namely a masculine, heroic father-figure and a soothing, protective mother-figure, respectively. It is a sad footnote of our contemporary society that these unresolved conflicts perpetuate themselves, and the adolescent sons and daughters who grow up in a psychological vacuum wrought by these conflicts, void of love and guidance, may embark on a similar cycle in their own adult lives, inflicting the same pattern on their own children (Adams, 1979; Bengtson and Troll, 1978; Petersen and Hamburg, 1986; Rutter, 1980; Steinberg, 1981; Youniss and Smollar, 1985).

DISTORTED PARENTHOOD

People who get married in order to get love and protection without being able or willing to give the same in return are not ready for a mature parenthood. Some of them, disappointed in their spouses, reject their children, thus starting them on the road toward maladjustment, antisocial behavior, and delinquency. Adolescents brought up in an unloving environment have little chance for identification and development of moral adjustment, and many of them become selfish and self-righteous (Montemayer, 1983; Wolman, 1987; Youniss and Smollar, 1985).

Some parents, disappointed in each other, expect emotional support from the child which the child is unable to give them. They exploit the child emotionally, robbing them of their childhood, using the child as a substitute for a disappointing spouse and forcing it into a morbid state of social role reversal; the adolescent is expected to worry about the parent and satisfy the parents' emotional needs (Steinberg, 1981, 1985). These "children without childhood" may become severely disturbed adolescents (Goldstein, 1988; Wolman, 1970).

Some parents vacillate in their attitudes and are highly inconsistent in their behavior. They view their children as a burden and are hostile to them, but every so often, ridden by feelings of guilt, they shower the rejected child with love, pity, and affection. The confused child may develop swinging moods of feeling rejected and depressed, or accepted and elated (Rutter, Izard, and Read, 1986).

Many people, feeling inadequate as parents, try to compensate for their shortcomings by becoming overprotective or overpermissive. Excessive permissiveness, which gives the child no sense of direction or moral guidance, seems to be more prevalent today than overprotectiveness, which infantalizes the child and delays psychological maturity (Adelson, 1980; Blos, 1979; Hetherington, 1983; Montemayer, 1983).

Immature parents are, as a rule, unfair to each other and act in an irresponsible manner toward their children. Quite often they wish to get rid of their difficult adolescent children and sometimes act in a hostile manner toward them. This parental hostility may be covert or overt. Some parents do hate their teenage children and punish them for true or imaginary transgressions.

In some parents, the fact that their teenage children are soon to become adults often elicits painful feelings of regret for the years wasted in quarrels and misery, and a fear of old age. People who would like to regress to childhood obviously abhor the idea of becoming grandparents. They may attempt to keep a young adult from leaving home by making them economically dependent (Steinberg, 1981; Wolman and Stricker, 1983). Thus, while some parents express the wish to see their children leave home and start their own families, their actions deny their pronouncements.

BROKEN HOMES

Divorce creates additional problems for adolescents. A two-parent family enables the growing children to resolve their Oedipal complexes and follow the appropriate psychosexual role model. The single-parent family has become a frequent occurrence, and in most instances the children live with their mothers (Dornbusch et al., 1985; Hetherington, 1983).

Adolescent girls who have lost their fathers through divorce or death often experience anxiety in the presence of males. Many of them seek attention and become overly dependent on male approval. Some of them are inclined to start early heterosexual behavior, and some develop subservient attitudes to their male partners.

The absence of a father impairs the boy's male identification process. Many of them, missing the appropriate male model, identify with their mothers. In some cases they develop homosexual behavior patterns (Deaux and Major, 1987; Dornbusch et al., 1985; Dreyer, 1982; Wolman and Stricker, 1983).

BEYOND ADOLESCENCE

Adolescent boys and girls who wish to become physicists, biochemists, physicians, engineers, psychologists, or experts in finance, law, architecture, and medicine need years of training well beyond their high school education (Super, 1984; Vondracek and Lerner, 1982; Walsh and Osipow, 1986). Farm hands or menial workers can start earning a living in their late teens, but future nuclear physicists and neurosurgeons require prolonged training, which means prolonged dependency.

To learn means to *depend* on those who teach. Those who study need support from their parents or society at large. Students do not enjoy the same social status as their professors; professors assign work, lecture, and examine, and students are ordered and judged by them. This inequality is inherent in the educational system.

University students, especially in higher classes and in graduate programs, are young adults. Most of them have left behind their adolescent immaturity, negativism, and rebelliousness. They are capable of participating as equals in interpersonal relationships and of tenacious pursuit of their goals (Pervin, 1988). However, due to the fact that they aspire to reach higher academic levels, they are compelled to continue their dependent role.

There is, indeed, some analogy regarding the relationship between an adult student and his or her instructor, and an adult patient and his or her therapist. A patient can be more intelligent than the doctor and certainly more competent in particular areas. I have had as patients lawyers, business executives, physicians, dentists, and engineers, who definitely knew more about their fields than I shall ever know. Yet the fact that they *needed my help* made them dependent on me, even when they were older and more competent than myself.

A professor of chemistry may have in his or her class students who are more gifted than himself. Some may be creative writers, musicians, and inventors. Yet they *need the professor's help* in chemistry and are, therefore, dependent on his or her competence and educational skills.

This dependence is not limited to the classroom situation. Full-time students cannot be gainfully employed or, at least, they can hardly support themselves adequately. Thus, while their peers, who are intellectually average, are economically adult, the brightest group of young adults has to continue to receive financial support from without.

It comes as no surprise, then, that some young people who are otherwise adult, but whose life conditions perpetuate childhood dependence, may develop *the overstayed adolescence syndrome*. This is the paradox of higher education; while preparing young people to attain the highest possible level of adjustment, higher education perpetuates the conflict between two social roles, one determined by one's physical and sexual maturity and the other related to one's inability to attain a full and responsible participation in adult life (Coleman, 1974; McEllroy, 1985).

This *prolonged adolescent* dependence is aggravated by the fact that the conflict comes at a time when one's intellectual development warrants a full participation in all aspects of adult life. It is further accentuated by the fact that while college students are usually brighter than their peers and more aware of current social, cultural, and economic issues, they exercise *less* control over their lives than their non-college peers. Working youth can join a labor union in a struggle against the employer; student organizations, however, have little influence on planning and guiding life on the campus. The institutions of higher learning are usually governed by social appointees and faculty who bestow upon the students the benefits of learning *without giving the students the right to have even a consulting voice in matters concerning their future.* Certainly students cannot assume the role of professors, but they resent being treated as if they had nothing to say about their future careers.

It cannot be surprising that a great many college students resent being treated as children when they are not children any longer. Most of them cope with this problem in a rational way without regressing into second adolescence. Some, however, act in a way which resembles the adolescent rebellion against authority, get carried away with it, and act in a destructive manner. Although the process of self-assertion is a product of normal growth, exaggerated and unrealistic plans, demands for excessive liberties, use of force, and outbursts of violence may be indicative of psychopathology (Wolman, 1973b, 1982b, 1987).

CHAPTER 17

Between
Adults and Adolescents

"MARGINAL MEN"

Kurt Lewin, a keen observer of social relations, described the peculiar situation of adolescents in this country. While adolescents are no longer children, they are only partly accepted by the ruling social group: the adults. The American adolescent has a position somewhat similar to what is called in sociology, "the marginal man."

> To some extent, behavior symptomatic for the marginal man can be found in the adolescent. He too is oversensitive, easily shifted from one extreme to the other. . . . He does not wish to belong any longer to a group which is, after all, less privileged than the group of adults; but at the same time he knows that he is not fully accepted by the adults. (Lewin, 1951)

Some American adults use derogatory terms in describing adolescents. There are many other cultures which do not share this attitude. Poets have described the idealism of youth, their zeal in serving their country and their readiness for self-sacrifice. The histories of ancient Judea, Greece, Rome, and other countries are full of heroic descriptions that depict youth as volunteers in defense, hard labor, and service for their compatriots. It seems that the adult society alienates the adolescent instead of helping them to take over the existing cultural values and the democratic social system. Bandura (1964) wrote as follows:

> If a society labels its adolescents as "teenagers," and expects them to be rebellious, unpredictable, sloppy and wild in their behavior, and if this picture is repeatedly reinforced by mass media, such cultural expectations may very

well force adolescents into the role of rebels. In this way, a false expectation may serve to instigate and maintain a certain role behavior in turn that reinforces the original false belief.

A great many problems of contemporary adolescence stem from the growing distance between the speed of biological and psychosocial development. The biological development, due to the "secular trend," comes earlier. Today's adolescents attain biological maturity earlier than their parents did, and much earlier than their grandparents and great-grandparents. At the same time, due to complex technological developments, they are less prepared to join the fabric of contemporary commitments and social relations of the adult society. They need more time, and definitely more education, to be able to earn a living and become responsible marital partners, parents, and members of society at large.

The frequent dissatisfaction of the adult society with adolescents is chiefly related to the fact that adolescents would like to be accepted as adults, whereas adolescent behavior is far from mature. The adult society is quite concerned with the frequent cases of maladjustment described in Part II of the present book, but it is not very successful in dealing with them. Psychotherapy is not a solution for a major social problem.

Psychotherapy deals with individuals and their mental health, as well as their mental disorders. It is a task of psychiatry and clinical psychology, and current research analyzes the best available and most efficient therapeutic methods. Adolescence is a biological and psycbosocial issue of transition from childhood to adulthood, but it is not psychopathology. The search for a rational solution must go beyond psychotherapy and concentrate on the discrepancy between biological and psychosocial development. It is impossible to slow down biological development, but it is possible and perhaps necessary to speed up psychosocial development.

SOCIAL RESPONSIBILITY

The adult society must not shy away from the problems partially created by its own way of life and its own sociocultural institutions. To confront angry young men with angry old men can only increase the existing tensions. An adult society which sways from extreme authoritarianism and punitive reactions to a pseudoliberal and noncommittal lack of guidance is not offering any means of solving the problem. The adult society often fails to see youth in perspective, and ignores the fact that in every generation young people strive to add their share to the existing sociocultural fabric. No society and no generation has found a final solution for problems that perplex humanity, and every effort to review old approaches and try new methods should be made welcome.

The trouble lies therefore not in the rebellions against tradition, but in the disruptive nature of present-day rebellions. Radical slogans do not necessarily represent justice, and forces of brutality, once unleashed, follow their own logic of destruction. Misguided youth may go astray, and unchecked adolescent outbursts may end in crimes against humanity.

Youth needs consideration; *young people need the opportunity to participate in planning their own futures and the opportunity to partake in public life in general.* Their abundant energies and spirit of enterprise could find constructive outlets. The adult society can offer help and guidance to the perplexed young generation.

References

Abelson, R.P. (1972). Are attitudes necessary? In B.T. King and E. McGinnies (Eds.), *Attitudes, Conflict and Social Change*. New York: Academic Press.

Adams, J.F. (Ed.) (1979). *Understanding Adolescence: Current Developments in Adolescent Psychology*. Boston: Allyn and Bacon.

Adams, N.M. (1964). Street of no remorse: What kind of people are we? *New York Journal American*.

Adelson, J.L. (Ed.) (1980). *Handbook of Psychology of Adolescence*. New York: New York Academy of Sciences.

Adelson, J.L., and Doehrman, M.J. (1980). The psychodynamic approach to adolescence. In J.L. Adelson (Ed.), *Handbook of Psychology of Adolescence*. New York: New York Academy of Sciences.

Ader, R. (Ed.) (1981). *Psychoneuroimmunology*. New York: Academic Press.

Adler, L.L. (1982). Cross-cultural research and theory. In B.B. Wolman (Ed.), *Handbook of Developmental Psychology*. Englewood Cliffs, NJ: Prentice-Hall.

Adler, L.L. (Ed.) (1977). *Issues in Cross-Cultural Research*. New York: New York Academy of Sciences.

Ajzen, L., and Fishbein, M. (1977). Attitude-behavior relations: A theoretical analysis and review of empirical research. *Psychological Bulletin*, 84, 888–918.

Anthony, E.J. (1979). The reactions of adults to adolescents and their behavior. In G. Kaplan and S. Lebovici (Eds.), *Adolescence: Psychosocial Perspectives*. New York: Basic Books.

Aries, P. (1962). *Centuries of Childhood: A Social History of Family Life*. New York: Random House.

Astin, H.S. (1985). The meaning of work in women's lives: A sociopsychological model of career choice and work behavior. *Counseling Psychology*, 12, 117–126.

Baker, T.B., and Cannon, D. (Eds.) (1987). *Addictive Behavior: Psychological Research on Assessment and Treatment*. New York: Praeger.

Baltes, P.B. (1973). Prototypcial paradigms and questions in life-span research on development and aging. *Gerontologist*, 13, 458–567.

Baltes, P.B., Reese, H.W., and Lipsitt, L.P. (1980). Life-span developmental psychology. *Annual Review of Psychology*, 31, 65–110.

Bandura, A. (1964). The stormy decade: Fact or fiction? *Psychology in the Schools*, 1, 224–231.

Bandura, A. (1973). *Aggression: A Social Learning Analysis*. Englewood Cliffs, NJ: Prentice-Hall.

Bandura, A. (1982). Self-efficacy mechanism in human agency. *American Psychologist*, 37, 122–147.

Bandura, A., and Walters, R. (1963). *Social Learning and Personality Development*. New York: Holt, Rinehart and Winston.

Beech, R.P., and Schoeppe, A. (1974). Development of value systems in adolescents. *Developmental Psychology*, 10, 644–656.

Beilin, H. (1976). Constructing cognitive operations linguistically. In H. Reese (Ed.), *Advances in Child Development and Behavior*. New York: Academic Press.

Bengtson, V.L., and Troll, L. (1978). Youth and their parents: Feedback and intergenerational influences. In R.M. Lerner and G.B. Spanier (Eds.), *Child Influences on Marital and Family Interaction: A Life-Span Perspective*. New York: Academic Press.

Bihari, B. (1976). Drug dependency: Some etiological considerations. *American Journal of Drug and Alcohol Abuse*, 3, 409–419

Binder, A. (1988). Juvenile delinquency. *Annual Review of Psychology*, 39, 252–282.

Biner, D.M. (1987). Effects of difficulty and goal value on goal valence. *Journal of Research in Personality*, 21, 395–404.

Blane, H.T., and Leonard, K.E. (Eds.) (1987). *Psychological Theories of Drinking and Alcoholism*. New York: Guilford.

Blos, P. (1970). *The Young Adolescent*. New York: Free Press.

Blos, P. (1979). *The Adolescent Passage*. New York: International Universities Press.

Bronfenbrenner, U. (1970). *Two Worlds of Childhood: USA and USSR*. New York: Russell Sage Foundation.

Bronfenbrenner, U. (1979). *The Ecology of Human Development: Experiments by Nature and Design*. Cambridge, MA: Harvard University Press.

Brooks-Gunn, J., and Petersen, A.C. (Eds.) (1983). *Girls at Puberty: Biological and Psychological Perspectives*. New York: Plenum.

Cadoret, R.J., Cain, C.A., and Grove, W.M. (1980). Development of alcoholism in adoptees raised apart from alcoholic biologic relatives. *Archives of General Psychiatry*, 37, 561–563.

Carper, J. (1987). *Health Care U.S.A.* New York: Prentice-Hall.

Carron, A.V., and Bailey, D.A. (1974). Strength development in boys from 10 to 16. *Monographs of the Society for Research in Child Development*, 39, 1–39.

Carson, R.C. (1989). Personality. *Annual Review of Psychology*, 40, 227–248.

Carter, E.A. and Goldrich, M. (Eds.) (1980). *The Family Life Circle*. New York: Gardner Press.

Cattell, R.B. (1982). *The Inheritance of Personality and Ability: Research Methods and Findings*. New York: Academic Press.

Cheek, D.B. (1974). Body composition, hormones, nutrition, and growth. In M.M.

Grumbach, G.D. Grave, and E.E. Mayer (Eds.), *Control of the Onset of Puberty.* New York: Wiley.

Chilman, C. (1979). *Adolescent Sexuality in a Changing American Society: Social and Psychological Perspectives.* New York: Wiley.

Chilman, C.S. (1978). *Adolescent Sexuality in a Changing American Society: Social and Psychological Perspectives.* Department of Health, Education and Welfare Publication 79-1426. Washington, DC: U.S. Government Printing Office.

Chumlea, D.B. (1982). Physical growth in adolescence. In B.B. Wolman (Ed.), *Handbook of Developmental Psychology.* Englewood Cliffs, NJ: Prentice-Hall.

Cloninger, C. and Reich, T. (1983). Genetic heterogenity in alcoholism and sociopathy. In S. Kety, L. Rowland, R. Sidman, and S. Mathysse (Eds.), *Genetics of Neurological and Psychiatric Disorders.* New York: Raven.

Coates, T.J., Peterson, A.C., and Perry, C. (Eds.) (1982). *Promoting Adolescent Health.* New York: Academic Press.

Coleman, J.S. (Ed.) (1974). *Youth: Transition to Adulthood.* Chicago: University of Chicago Press.

Conger, J.J., and Miller, W.C. (1966). *Personality, Social Class and Delinquency.* New York: Wiley.

Conger, J.J., and Petersen, A.C. (1984). *Adolescence and Youth.* New York: Harper and Row.

Cooper, C., Grotevant, H., and Condon, S. (1983). Individuality and connectedness in the family as a context for adolescent identity formation and role-taking skills. In H. Grotevant and C. Cooper (Eds.), *Adolescent Development in the Family.* San Francisco: Jossey-Bass.

Crosby, F. (1982). *Relative Deprivation and Working Women.* New York: Oxford University Press.

Damon, W., and Hart, D. (1982). The development of self-understanding from infancy through adolescence. *Child Development*, 53, 841–864.

Datan, N., and Reese, H.W. (Eds.) (1977). *Life-Span Developmental Psychology: Dialectical Perspectives on Experimental Research.* New York: Academic Press.

Deaux, K. and Major, B. (1987). Putting gender into context: An interactive model of gender-related behavior. *Psychological Review*, 94, 369–389.

De Beauvoir, S. (1953). *The Second Sex.* New York: Knopf.

Deutsch, H. (1945). *The Psychology of Women: A Psychoanalytic Interpretation.* New York: Grune and Stratton.

Diepold, J., and Young, R.D. (1979). Empirical studies of adolescent sexual behavior. *Adolescence*, 14, 45–64.

Dornbusch, S.M., Carlsmith, J.M., Bushwall, S.J., Ritter, P.L., Leiderman, H., Hastorf, A.H., and Gross, R.T. (1985). Single parents, extended households, and the control of adolescents. *Child Development*, 56, 326–341.

Douvan, E., and Adelson, J. (1966). *The Adolescent Experience.* New York: Wiley.

Drake, C.T., and McDougall, D. (1977). Effects of the absence of the father and other male models on the development of boys' sex roles. *Developmental Psychology*, 13, 537–539.

Dreyer, P.H. (1982). Sexuality during adolescence. In B.B. Wolman (Ed.), *Handbook of Developmental Psychology.* Englewood Cliffs, NJ: Prentice-Hall.

Edwards, V.J., and Spence, J.T. (1987). Gender related traits, stereotypes, and schemata. *Journal of Personality and Social Psychology*, 53, 146–154.

Ember, C.R. (1981). A cross-cultural perspective on sex differences. In R.H. Munroe, R.L. Munroe, and B.B Whiting (Eds.), *Handbook of Cross-Cultural Human Development*. New York: Garland Press.

Erikson, E.H. (1968). *Identity: Youth and Crisis*. New York: Norton.

Eveleth, P.B., and Tanner, J.M. (1976). *World-Wide Variation in Human Growth*. Cambridge, England: Cambridge University Press.

Falkner, F., and Tanner, J.M. (Eds.) (1978). *Human Growth*. New York: Plenum.

Farmer, H.S. (1983). Career and homemaking plans for high school youth. *Journal of Counseling Psychology*, 30, 40–45.

Farmer, H.S. (1985). Model of career and achievement motivation for women and men. *Journal of Counseling Psychology*, 32, 363–390.

Fassinger, R.E. (1985). A causal model of college women's career choice. *Journal of Vocational Behavior*, 27, 123–153.

Faust, M.S. (1983). Alternative constructions of adolescent growth. In J. Brooks-Gunn and A.C. Petersen (Eds.), *Girls at Puberty: Biological and Psychosocial Perspectives*. New York: Plenum.

Feather, N.T. (1980). Values in adolescence. In J. Adelson (Ed.), *Handbook of Adolescent Psychology*. New York: Wiley.

Flavell, J.H., and Markman, E.M. (1983). *Handbook of Child Psychology: Cognitive Development*. New York: Wiley.

Fleck, S. (1983). Family and mental health. In B.B. Wolman (Ed.), *International Encyclopedia of Psychiatry, Psychology, Psychoanalysis and Neurology*, Progress Volume 1. New York: Aesculapius Publishers.

Freud, A. (1946). *The Psychoanalytic Treatment of Children*. London: Imago Publishing.

Freud, A. (1958). *Adolescence: Psychoanalytic Study of the Child*. Vol. 13. New York: International Universities Press.

Freud, S. (1932). *New Introductory Lectures on Psychoanalysis*. New York: Norton.

Freud, S. (1938). *An Outline of Psychoanalysis*. New York: Norton.

Fuller, J.L., and Simmell, E.C. (1983). *Behavior Genetics: Principles and Applications*. Hillsdale, NJ: Erlbaum.

Gaeddert, W.P. (1987). The relationship of gender, gender-related traits and achievement attributions: A study of subject selected accomplishments. *Journal of Personality*, 55, 687–710.

Garner, D.M., and Garfinkel, P.E. (1980). Sociocultural factors in the development of anorexia nervosa. *Psychological Medicine*, 10, 647–656.

Goldberger, A.S. (1978). Pitfalls in the resolution of IQ inheritance. In N.E. Morton and C.S. Chung (Eds.), *Genetic Epidemiology*. New York: Academic Press.

Goldstein, A.P., and Segall, M.H. (1983). *Aggression in Global Perspective*. Elmsford, NY: Pergamon.

Goldstein, M.J. (1988). Family and psychopathology. *Annual Review of Psychology*, 39, 283–299.

Green, L.W., and Horton, D. (1982). Adolescent health: Issues and challenges. In T.J. Coates, A.C. Petersen, and C. Perry (Eds.), *Promoting Adolescent Health: A Dialogue on Research and Practice*. New York: Academic Press.

Grotevant, H., and Cooper, C. (1985). Patterns of interaction in family relationships and the development of identity exploration in adolescence. *Child Development*, 56, 415–428.

Grotevant, H., and Cooper, C. (1986). Individuation in family relationships. *Human Development*, 29, 82–100.

Grotevant, H., and Cooper, C. (Eds.) (1983). *Adolescent Developments in the Family*. San Francisco: Jossey-Bass.

Grumbach, M.M., Grave, G.D., and Mayer, E.E. (Eds.) (1974). *Control of the Onset of Puberty*. New York: Wiley.

Gurling, H., Oppenheim, B., and Murray, R. (1984). Depression, criminality, and psychopathology associated with alcoholism: Evidence from a twin study. *Acta Genetica Medica*, 33, 333–339.

Hall, G.S. (1904). *Adolescence*. New York: Appleton-Century-Crofts.

Hamburg, B.A. (1974). Early adolescence: A specific and stressful stage of the life cycle. In G.V. Coelho and J.E. Adams (Eds.), *Coping and Adaptation*. New York: Basic Books.

Hart, H.L. (1974). Gonadal androgen and sociosexual behavior of male mammals: A comparative analysis. *Psychological Bulletin*, 81, 383–409.

Hass, A. (1979). *Teenage Sexuality, a Survey of Teenage Sexual Behavior*. New York: Macmillan.

Hauser, S.T., Powers, S.I., Noam, G.G., Jacobson, A.M., Weiss, B., and Follansbee, D.J. (1984). Familial contexts of adolescent ego development. *Child Development*, 55, 195–213.

Henry, J., and Henry, Z. (1953). Doll play in Pilaga Indian children. In C. Kluckhorn and H.A. Murray (Eds.), *Personality in Nature, Society and Culture*. New York: Knopf.

Hetherington, E.M. (1983). Socialization, personality, and social development. In P.H. Mussen (Ed.), *Handbook of Child Psychology*. New York: Wiley.

Hogan, R., and Emler, R.H. (1978). Moral development. In M.E. Lamb (Ed.), *Social and Personality Development*. New York: Holt, Rinehart and Winston.

Holland, J.L. (1985). *Making Vocational Choices*. Englewood Cliffs, NJ: Prentice-Hall.

Hollingworth, L.S. (1928). *The Psychology of Adolescence*. Englewood Cliffs, NJ: Prentice-Hall.

Huba, G.H., and Bender, P.M. (1982). A developmental theory of drug use. In P.B. Baltes and O.G. Brim (Eds.), *Life-Span Development and Behavior*. New York: Academic Press.

Inhelder, B., and Piaget, J. (1958). *The Growth of Logical Thinking*. New York: Basic Books.

Jacob, T. (1975). Family interaction in disturbed and normal families: A methodological and substantive review. *Psychological Bulletin*, 82, 33–65.

Jacobs, J. (1971). *Adolescent Suicide*. New York: Wiley.

Jessor, R. (1984). Adolescent development and mental health. In J.D. Matarazzo, S.M. Weiss, J.A. Herd, N.E. Miller, and S.M. Weiss (Eds.), *Behavioral Health*. New York: Wiley.

Jessor, R., and Jessor, S. (1979). *Problem Behavior and Psychological Development*. New York: Academic Press.

Jessor, R., and Jessor, S.L. (1977). *Problem Development and Psychological Development*. New York: Academic Press.

Jessor, R.J., and Jessor, S.L. (1982). Adolescence to young adulthood: A twelve year prospective study of problem behavior and psychosocial development. In A.A. Mednick and M. Harvey (Eds.), *Longitudinal Research in the United States*. Boston: Nijhoff Press.

Jordaan, J.P., and Heyde, M.B. (1979). *Vocational Maturity During the High School Years*. New York: Teachers College Press.

Kandel, D.B., and Davies, M. (1982). Epidemiology of depressive mood in adolescence. *Archives of General Psychiatry*, 39, 1205–1212.

Kandel, D.B., and Lesser, G.S. (1972). *Youth in Two Worlds*. San Francisco: Jossey-Bass.

Kaplan, H.B. (1989). *Deviant Behavior in Defence of Self*. New York: Wiley.

Kaplan, S.L., Hong, G.K., and Weinhold, C. (1984). Epidemiology of depressive symptoms in adolescence. *Journal of American Academy of Child Psychiatry*, 23, 91–98.

Karplus, B. (1981). Education and formal thought—a modest proposal. In I. Siegel, D. Brodzinsky, and R. Golinkoff (Eds.), *Piagetian Theory and Research—New Directions and Applications*. Hillsdale, NJ: Erlbaum.

Katchadourian, H. (1977). *The Biology of Adolescence*. San Francisco: Freeman.

Keating, D.P., and Clark, L.V. (1980). Development of physical and social reasoning in adolescence. *Developmental Psychology*, 16, 23–30.

Kessler, R.C., and McLeod, J. (1985). Social support and psychological distress in community surveys. In S. Cohen and L. Syme (Eds.), *Social Support and Health*. New York: Academic Press.

Kiell, N. (1964). *The Universal Experience of Adolescence*. New York: International Universities Press.

Kinsey, A.C., Pomeroy, W.B., and Martin, C.E. (1948). *Sexual Behavior in the Human Male*. Philadelphia: Saunders.

Kinsey, A.C., Pomeroy, W.B., and Martin, C.E. (1953). *Sexual Behavior in the Human Female*. Philadelphia: Saunders.

Kircheisen, F.M. (Ed.) (1931). *Napoleon's Autobiography*. New York: Dodd, Mead.

Klineberg, O., Zavalloni, M., Louis-Guerinc, C., and Ben-Brika, J. (1979). *Students, Values and Politics: A Cross-Cultural Comparison*. New York: Free Press.

Kohlberg, L. (1976). Moral stages and moralization: The cognitive-developmental approach. In T. Lickona (Ed.), *Moral Development and Behavior*. New York: Holt, Rinehart and Winston.

Labouvie, E.W. (1982). Issues in life-span development. In B.B. Wolman (Ed.,) *Handbook of Developmental Psychology*. Englewood Cliffs, NJ: Prentice-Hall.

Lerner, R.M., and Busch-Rossnagel, N.A. (1981). Individuals as producers of their development: Conceptual and empirical bases. In R.M. Lerner and N.A. Busch-Rossnagel (Eds.), *Individuals as Producers of Their Development: A Life-Span Perspective*. New York: Academic Press.

Lerner, R.M., and Foch, T.T. (Eds.) (1987). *Biological-Psychosocial Interaction in Early Adolescence: A Life-Span Perspective*. Hillsdale, NJ: Erlbaum.

Lerner, R.M., and Shea, J.A. (1982). Social behavior in adolescence. In B.B. Wolman (Ed.), *Handbook of Develpmental Psychology*. Englewood Cliffs, NJ: Prentice-Hall.

Lerner, R.M., and Spanier, G.B. (Ed.) (1978). *Child Influences on Marital and Family Interaction: A Life-Span Perspective*. New York: Academic Press.

Lewin, K. (1951). *Field Theory in Social Science*. New York: Harper and Row.

Lewis, M., and Rosenblum, L.A. (1974). *The Effect of the Infant on Its Caregiver*. New York: Wiley.

Lidz, T. (1969). The adolescent and his family. In J. Kaplan and S. Lebovici (Eds.), *Adolescence: Psychosocial Perspectives*. New York: Basic Books.

Lipsitz, J. (1977). *Growing Up Forgotten: A Review of Research and Programs Concerning Early Adolescence.* Lexington, MA: Heath.

Loehlin, J.C., Willerman, L., and Horn, J.M. (1988). Human behavior genetics. *Annual Review of Psychology*, 39, 101–133.

Long, B.H., Henderson, E.H., and Platt, L. (1973). Self–other orientations of Israeli adolescents reared in kibbutzim and moshavim. *Developmental Psychology*, 8, 300–308.

Long, J.V.F., and Scherl, D.J. (1984). Developmental antecedents of compulsive drug use: A report on the literature. *Journal of Psychoactive Drugs*, 16, 169–182.

Lynd, R.S. (1946). *Knowledge for What.* Princeton, NJ: Princeton University Press.

Magnuson, D. (Ed.) (1987). *Series Paths Through Life.* Hillsdale, NJ: Erlbaum.

Malina, R.M. (1978). Adolescent growth and maturation: Selected aspects of current research. *Yearbook of Physical Anthropology*, 21, 63–94.

Manconi, L. (1980). *Vivere Con Il Terrorismo.* Milan, Italy: Arnoldo Mondadori.

Marshall, W.A., and Tanner, J.M. (1969). Variations in the pattern of pubertal changes in girls. *Archives of Disease in Childhood*, 44, 291–303.

Marshall, W.A., and Tanner, J.M. (1970). Variations in the pattern of pubertal changes in boys. *Archives of Disease in Childhood*, 45, 13–20.

Matarazzo, J.D., Weiss, S.M., Herd, J.A., Miller, N.E., and Weiss, S.M. (Eds.) (1984). *Behavioral Health.* New York: Wiley.

Matteson, D.R. (1974). Adolescent self-esteem, family communication and marital satisfaction. *Journal of Psychology*, 86, 35–47.

McEllroy, J.C. (1985). Inside the teaching machine: Integrating attribution and reinforcement theories. *Journal of Management*, 11, 123–141.

McKenry, P.C., Walters, L.H., and Johnson, C. (1979). Adolescent pregnancy: A review of the literature. *Family Coordination*, 28, 16–28.

McKinney, J.P., Hotch, D.F., and Truhon, S.A. (1977). The organization of behavioral values during late adolescence: Change and stability across two eras. *Developmental Psychology*, 13, 83–89.

Mead, M. (1949). *Male and Female: A Social History of Family Life.* New York: Morrow.

Mead, M. (1970). *Culture and Commitment: A Study of the Generation Gap.* New York: Doubleday.

Meyer, R.E. (Ed.) (1986). *Psychopathology and Addictive Behavior.* New York: Guilford Press.

Meyer-Bahlburg, H.F.L., Ehrhardt, A.A., Bell, J.J., Cohen, S.F., Healy, J.M., Feldman, J.F., Morishima, A., Baker, S.W., and New, M.J. (1985). Idiopathic precocious puberty in girls: Psychosexual development. *Journal of Youth Adolescence*, 14, 339–353.

Millman, R.B. (1978). Drug and alcohol abuse. In B.B. Wolman, J. Egan, and A.O. Ross (Eds.), *Treatment of Mental Disorders in Childhood and Adolescence.* Englewood Cliffs, NJ: Prentice-Hall.

Money, J. (1980). *Love and Lovesickness: The Science of Sex, Gender Difference, and Pair-Bounding.* Baltimore: John Hopkins Press.

Montemayer, R. (1983). Parents and adolescents in conflict: All families some of the time and some families most of the time. *Journal of Early Adolescence*, 3, 83–101.

Munroe, R.H., Munroe, R.L., and Whiting, B.B. (Eds.) (1981). *Handbook of Cross-Cultural Human Development.* New York: Garland Press.

Neimark, E.D. (1982). Adolescent thoughts: Transition to formal operations. In B.B. Wolman (Ed.), *Handook of Developmental Psychology.* Englewood Cliffs, NJ: Prentice-Hall.

Nesselrode, J.R., and Baltes, P.B. (Eds.) (1979). *Longitudinal Research in the Study of Behavior and Development*. New York: Academic Press.

Newman, P.R. (1982). The peer group. In B.B. Wolman (Ed.), *Handbook of Developmental Psychology*. Englewood Cliffs, NJ: Prentice-Hall.

Ochberg, F.M. (1982). Sociopolitical climate of contemporary terrorism. *International Journal of Group Tension*, 12, 62–83.

Offer, D and Offer, J. (1975). *From Teenager to Young Adulthood: A Psychological Study*. New York: Basic Books.

Olweus, D. (1979). Stability of aggressive reaction patterns in males: A review. *Psychological Bulletin*, 86, 852–875.

Osofsky, J.D. (Ed.) (1979). *Handbook of Infant Development*. New York: Wiley.

Ostrov, E., Offer, D., and Howard, J.K. (1986). Cross-cultural sex differences in normal adolescents' self-image. *Hillside Journal of Clinical Psychiatry*, 8, 183–192.

Pascual-Leone, J. (1980). Constructive problems for constructive theories: The current relevance of Piaget's work and a critique of information processing stimulation psychology. In H. Spada and R. Kluwe (Eds.), *Developmental Models of Thinking*. New York: Academic Press.

Pattison, E.M., and Kaufman, E. (Eds.) (1982). *Encyclopedic Handbook of Alcoholism*. New York: Gardner Press.

Perez, J.F. (1978). *The Family Roots of Adolescent Delinquency*. New York: Van Nostrand Reinhold.

Pervin, L. (Ed.) (1988). *Goal Concepts in Personality and Social Psychology*. Hillsdale, NJ: Erlbaum.

Peskin, H. (1973). Influence of the developmental schedule of puberty and ego functioning. *Journal of Youth and Adolescence*, 2, 273–290.

Petersen, A.C. (1979). Female pubertal development. In M. Sugar (Ed.), *Female Adolescent Development*. New York: Brunner/Mazel.

Petersen, A.C. (1988). Adolescent development. *Annual Review of Psychology*, 39, 583–607.

Petersen, A.C., and Crocket, L.J. (1985). Pubertal timing and grade effects on adjustment. *Journal of Youth and Adolescence*, 14, 191–206.

Petersen, A.C. and Ebata, A.T. (1988). Developmental transitions and adolescent problem behavior: Implications for prevention and intervention. In K. Hurrelman (Ed.), *Social Prevention and Intervention*. New York: De Gruyter.

Petersen, A.C., and Hamburg, B.A. (1986). Adolescence: A developmental approach to problems and psychopatholgy. *Behavior Therapy*, 17, 480–499.

Petersen, A.C., and Seligman, M.E.P. (1984). Causal explanations as a risk for depression: Theory and evidence. *Psychological Review*, 91, 347–374.

Petersen, A.C., and Spiga, R. (1982). Adolescence and stress. In L. Goldberger and S. Bresnitz (Eds.), *Handbook of Stress: Theoretical and Clinical Aspects*. New York: Free Press.

Piaget, J. (1952). *The Origins of Intelligence in Children*. New York: International Universities Press.

Piaget, J. (1965). *The Moral Judgment of the Child*. New York: Free Press.

Quay, H.C. (Ed.) (1987). *Handbook of Juvenile Delinquency*. New York: Wiley.

Rabin, A.I. (1983). Personality development in the Israeli kibbutz. In B.B. Wolman (Ed.), *International Encyclopedia of Psychiatry, Psychology, Psychoanalysis and Neurology*. First Progress Volume. New York: Aesculapius.

Raine, C.S. (Ed.) (1988). *Advances in Neuroimmunology*. New York: New York Academy of Sciences.

Rainwater, L. (1970). *Behind Ghetto Walls: Black Families in a Federal Slum*. Chicago: Aldine.

Reis, H.T., and Shaver, R. (1989). Intimacy as an interpersonal process. In S. Duck (Ed.), *Handbook of Personal Relationships: Theory, Relationships and Interventions*. New York: Wiley.

Roche, A.F. (Ed.) (1979). Secular trends in growth, maturation and development of children. *Monographs of the Society for Research in Child Development*, 44, 3–27.

Rokeach, M. (Ed.) (1979). *Understanding Human Values*. New York: Free Press.

Rose, R.J., and Ditto, W.B. (1983). A developmental-genetic analysis of common fears from early adolescence to early adulthood. *Child Development*, 54, 361–368.

Rosenthal, A.M. (1964). A study of a sickness called apathy. *New York Times*, May 3.

Ruble, D.N., and Brooks-Gunn, J. (1982). The experience of menarche. *Child Development*, 53, 1557–1566.

Rutter, M. (1980). *Changing Youth in a Changing Society: Patterns of Adolescent Development and Disorder*. Cambridge, MA: Harvard University Press.

Rutter, M., Izard, C., and Read, P. (Eds.) (1986). *Depression in Young People: Developmental and Clinical Perspectives*. New York: Guilford Press.

Santrock, J.W. (1987). *Adolescence: An Introduction*. Dubuque, IA: Brown.

Schuckitt, M.A. (1987). Biological vulnerability to alcoholism. *Journal of Consulting and Clinical Psychology*, 55, 301–309.

Schweitzer, A. (1950). *Memories of Childhood and Youth*. New York: Macmillan.

Segall, M.H. (1986). Culture and behavior. *Annual Review of Psychology*, 37, 523–564.

Seligman, M.E.P., and Peterson, C. (1986). A learned helplessness perspective on childhood depression: Theory and research. In M. Rutter, C. Izard, and P. Read (Eds.), *Depression in Young People: Developmental and Clinical Perspectives*. New York: Guilford Press.

Shepherd-Look, D.L. (1982). Sex differentiation and the development of sex roles. In B.B. Wolman (Ed.), *Handbook of Developmental Psychology*. Englewood Cliffs, NJ: Prentice-Hall.

Shiffman, S., and Wills, T.A. (Eds.) (1985). *Coping and Substance Use*. New York: Academic Press.

Siegel, O. (1982). Personality development in adolescence. In B.B. Wolman (Ed.), *Handbook of Developmental Psychology*. Englewood Cliffs, NJ: Prentice-Hall.

Simmons, R.G., and Blyth, D.A. (1988). *Moving into Adolescence: The Impact of Pubertal Change and School Context*. New York: Aldine.

Simmons, R.G., Blyth, D.A., and McKinney, K.L. (1983). The social and psychological effects of puberty on white females. In J. Brooks-Gunn and A.C. Petersen (Eds.), *Girls at Puberty: Biological and Psychosocial Perspectives*. New York: Plenum.

Sinclair, D. (1978). *Human Growth after Birth*. London: Oxford University Press.

Smith, T.E. (1976). Push and pull: Intra-family versus peer-group variables as possible determinants of adolescent orientation toward parents. *Youth and Society*, 8, 5–26.

Steinberg, L.D. (1981). Transformation in family relations at puberty. *Developmental Psychology*, 7, 833–840.

Steinberg, L.D. (1985). *Adolescence*. New York: Knopf.

Super, D.E. (1984). Career life and development. In D. Brown and L. Brooks (Eds.), *Career Choice Development*. San Francisco: Jossey-Bass.

Taifel, H., and Turner, J.C. (1986). An integrative theory of intergroup relations. In S. Worchel and W.G. Austin (Eds.), *Psychology of Intergroup Relations*. Chicago: Nelson-Hall.

Tanner, J.M. (1974). Sequence and tempo in the somatic changes in puberty. In M.M. Grumbach, G.D. Grave, and P.E. Mayer (Eds.), *Control of the Onset of Puberty*. New York: Wiley.

Unger, R.K., and Denmark, F.L. (Eds.) (1975). *Woman: Dependent or Independent Variable?* New York: Psychological Dimensions.

Vaillant, G.E. (1983). *The Natural History of Alcoholism*. Cambridge, MA: Harvard University Press.

Vandenberg, S.G., and Vogler, G.P. (1985). Genetic determinants of intelligence. In B.B. Wolman (Ed.), *Handbook of Intelligence: Theories, Measurements and Applications*. New York: Wiley.

Van Hasselt, V.B., and Hersen, M. (Eds.) (1987). *Handbook of Adolescent Psychology*. New York: Pergamon.

Vondracek, F.W., and Lerner, R.M. (1982). Vocational role in adolescence. In B.B. Wolman (Ed.) *Handbook of Developmental Psychology*. Englewood Cliffs, NJ: Prentice-Hall.

Walsh, W.B., and Osipow, S.H. (Eds.) (1986). *Handbook of Vocational Psychology*. Hillsdale, NJ: Erlbaum.

Warren, N. (Ed.) (1977). *Studies in Cross-Cultural Psychology*. New York: Academic Press.

Weiner, I.B., and DelGaudio, A. (1976). Psychopathology in adolescence. *Archives of General Psychiatry*, 33, 187–193.

Weiner, J.B. (1970). *Psychological Disturbance in Adolescence*. New York: Wiley.

Weissman, M.M., and Klerman, G.L. (1977). Sex differences and the epidemiology of depression. *Archives of General Psychiatry*, 34, 98–111.

West, D.J., and Farrington, D.P. (1977). *Who Becomes Delinquent?* London: Heineman Educational.

Williams, R.H. (Ed.) (1979). *Textbook of Endocrinology*. Philadelphia: Saunders.

Wilson, J.Q., and Herrnstein, R.J. (1985). *Crime and Human Nature*. New York: Simon & Schuster.

Winter, D.G., and Stewart, A.J. (1978). Power motivation. In H. London and J. Exner (Eds.), *Dimensions of Personality*. New York: Wiley.

Winter, J.S. (1978). Prepubertal and pubertal endocrinology. In H. Reese (Ed.), *Human Growth*. New York: Plenum.

Wolman, B.B. (1970). *Children Without Childhood: A Study in Childhood Schizophrenia*. New York: Grune and Stratton.

Wolman, B.B. (1973a). *Call No Man Normal*. New York: International Universities Press.

Wolman, B.B. (1973b). The rebellion of youth. *International Journal of Social Psychiatry*, 18, 11–19.

Wolman, B.B. (1973c). Violent behavior. *International Journal of Group Tensions*, 3, 127–141.

Wolman, B.B. (1974). Power and acceptance as determinants of social relations. *International Journal of Group Tensions*, 4, 151–183.

Wolman, B.B. (1978a). *Children's Fears*. New York: Grosset and Dunlap.

Wolman, B.B. (Ed.) (1978b). *Psychological Aspects of Gynecology and Obstetrics*. Oradell, NJ: Medical Economics.

Wolman, B.B. (1982a). Interactional theory. In B.B. Wolman (Ed.), *Handbook of Developmental Psychology*. Englewood Cliffs, NJ: Prentice-Hall.

Wolman, B.B. (1982b). The followers. *International Journal of Group Tensions*, 12, 105–121.

Wolman, B.B. (1983). Deculturation and Disinhibition. In B.B. Wolman (Ed.), *International Encyclopedia for Psychiatry, Psychology, Psychoanalysis and Neurology*. Progress Volume 1. New York: Aesculapius Publishers.

Wolman, B.B. (1984a). *Interactional Psychotherapy*. New York: Van Nostrand Reinhold.

Wolman, B.B. (1984b). *Logic of Science in Psychoanalysis*. New York: Columbia University Press.

Wolman, B.B. (Ed.) (1985). *Handbook of Intelligence*. New York: Wiley.

Wolman, B.B. (1987). *The Sociopathic Personality*. New York: Brunner-Mazel.

Wolman, B.B. (1989). *Dictionary of Behavioral Science*. (2nd Ed.) New York: Academic Press.

Wolman, B.B. (in press). *Moral Behavior*.

Wolman, B.B., Egan, J., and Ross, A.O. (Eds.) (1978). *Handbook of Treatment of Mental Disorders in Childhood and Adolescence*. Englewood Cliffs, NJ: Prentice-Hall.

Wolman, B.B., and Krauss, H. (1976). *Between Survival and Suicide*. New York: Gardner.

Wolman, B.B., and Money, J. (Eds.) (1980). *Handbook of Human Sexuality*. Englewood Cliffs, NJ: Prentice-Hall.

Wolman, B.B., and Money, J. (Eds.) (1993). *Handbook of Human Sexuality*, 2nd ed. Northvale, NJ: Jason Aronson.

Wolman, B.B., and Stricker, G. (Eds.) (1983*). Handbook of Family and Marital Therapy*. New York: Plenum.

Yamaguchi, K., and Kandel, D.B. (1984). Patterns of drug use from adolescence to young adulthood. *American Journal of Public Health*, 74, 673–681.

Youniss, J., and Smollar, J. (1985). *Adolescent Relations with Mothers, Fathers and Friends*. Chicago: University of Chicago Press.

Zelnik, M., and Kantner, J.F. (1977). Sexual and contraceptive experience of young unmarried women. *Family Planning Perspectives*, 9, 55–71.

Zelnik, M., and Kantner, J.F. (1980). Sexual activity, contraceptive use and pregnancy among metropolitan teenagers. *Family Planning Perspectives*, 12, 230–237.

Zucker, R.A., and Gomberg, E.S.L. (1986). Etiology of alcoholism: The case for a biopsychosocial process. *American Psychologist*, 41, 783–793.

Index

About the Author

BENJAMIN B. WOLMAN is in private practice of psychoanalysis and psycho-therapy, and is the author and editor of numerous books on related subjects.